BIG DECISIONS ARE BEST MADE WITH HOT DOGS

JOE HUDSON

Copyright © 2013 Joe Hudson
All rights reserved.
ISBN: 1482375400
ISBN 13: 9781482375404
Library of Congress Control Number: 2013903402
CreateSpace Independent Publishing Platform
North Charleston, SC

Foreword

I was born and raised in eastern North Carolina and spent half of my life in a wonderful place called Hudson's Crossroads. One day I spread my wings, caught a strong westerly tailwind and landed in Statesville, North Carolina. I covered a lot of ground and along the way I wrote story songs in the hopes that one day I'd be a famous musician. The stories have survived. The guitar is somewhere in a closet downstairs in the house.

Many of the stories in this book have been published in my weekly newspaper column which has been published by our local newspaper for almost four years now. However, these stories are the complete version told without the constraint of word counts. I am grateful to the many readers that created the demand for this book and humbly submit this work to you for your pleasure.

We are told there is no new thing under the sun, and there is certainly nothing new in this book that has not been experienced by people everywhere unless they've spent their life in a mineshaft. Love, deceit, joy, fun, marriage, politics, relationships with friends and family, bird feeder problems, missing socks and even issues involved with cooking a pot of stew — it's all here.

These are stories about life, and therefore they have been told in one form or another by other people but it is amazing that though we all seem to have similar experiences, we each see them in a different light. This is my version of life so far.

This book is about you and me. I hope you enjoy reading it as much as I've enjoyed experiencing it.

Table of Contents

1. **Back Home Down East** 1
   Jack Daniels Kept Me from
      Jim Beam and Johnnie Walker 3
   Country Basketball 19
   Cucumbers Remind Me of Stars and Lora 29
   Gospel Music Led Me to Motorcycles 33
   My English Teacher Was
      Strict and She Smoked Cigars 37
   Oh Come to Me, My Sweet — Corn 41
   Sometimes You Have to
      Leave to Find Yourself 45
   A new look at family 49

2. **Holidays and Other Tribulations** 51
   A Dickens of a Christmas Tale 53
   Santa, Thanks for the Email 57
   It's Thanksgiving, Stop
      Texting and Give Thanks 61
   Thanksgiving Is About Tradition,
      God Help Us 65
   It's Over, So Button Your Pants 69
   Christmas and the Wonder of It All 73

Beware the Vacation, Pull Kudzu Instead *75*
An Old Testament View of Vacations *79*
Christmas in July
    Means Hamburgers and Garland. *81*

3. **Parents & Family** **85**
    The Wicked Daddy Giant and
        The Magic Cow *87*
    Mother's Love Is Not Sentimental. *91*
    Things Getting to You? Put On a Stew *95*
    My Mother Is an Iceberg *97*
    My Momma Rides
        Motorcycles and Plays Golf. *101*
    Confessions of an Empty Nester *105*
    My Cousin, My Brother. *107*
    A Report Card for Adults. *109*
    Missing Socks — They Want a Life *113*

4. **Traveling** **117**
    Daddy Hugs Away the Nightmares *119*
    When In a Marriage, Plans Change. *123*
    The Young Never Change,
        Thank Goodness. *127*
    The World Needs More
        Southern Gentlemen *131*
    I'm Motorcycling Out of Father's Day *133*
    Be Pleasant, Be Sweet, Be Southern! *135*

5. **Food** **137**
    Big Decisions Are Best Made
        with Hot Dogs *139*
    Grilling Is a Southern Family Sport *143*
    It's Spring, Forget Politics and
        Think Banana Pudding. *147*
    Baked Beans May Save the Family *151*
    We Need to Bake More Cakes *155*
    I Don't KitchenAid Anymore *159*

6. **Marriage and Other Daily Experiences** **163**
   February and Hot Flashes
      Can Freeze a Man. *165*
   Ferdinand Magellan and Me. *167*
   What is life all about?. *169*
   Arresting Thoughts While Driving *173*
   All You Need is Love at High Volume *175*
   Local Man Seeks Solitude,
      Claims to Be Normal. *177*
   Life Is Unfair and the
      Trash Has to Be Taken Out *179*
   Let's Joke Around. *181*
   I Saw a Real Parent at Burger King *183*
   The High Price of Togetherness. *185*
   Her Boots Are the First to Hit the Ground *189*
   You Can Get It Together at the Stoplight *193*
   Draw On Your Ear and Sing Like a Viking. *195*
   Domesticated Caveman
      Fuzzy on the Details. *197*
   Doctor, I'm Tired of Pulling the Plow *201*
   Becoming a Cowboy — the Nu-Way *203*
   The Diet of a Pharisee *205*
   The Day My Barber Left Town *207*

7. **The Animals in My Life** **209**
   When It Snows I Carry a Mule. *211*
   The Devil Wears Fur and
      Watches Desperate Housewives *213*
   Bureaucracy Got the Bull *217*
   Squirrel Threatens Nice Man
      Over Birdfeeder. *221*
   Building a Nest Calls for Compromise. *225*

8. **The Sweet & Funny of Life**. **227**
   A Quick Glimpse Over the Edge *229*
   A New Laptop Computer
      Brings Me in Line. *233*

Men Should Do as They Are Told,
    It's Cheaper *235*
Man Ponders Mortality Under a Car *239*
I'll Take Two Hamburgers
    without the Palm Trees *241*
Kisses Sweeter Than — Mustard *245*
Hard Work Teaches You a
    Song and the Way Home *247*
Free Therapy and Inner Peace,
    Right Here! *249*
For All the Waiting People of the World *251*
The Class of 1971 Has
    My Heart — and My Stomach *253*
Blue Skies and Each
    Individual Leaf Is a Wonder *255*
The Taming of a Man. *259*
Soap or Consequences *261*
Sir, Your Screams Are Forgiven *263*
Sex in the Secret Service
    Reminds Me of Superman *267*
Please Tell Me Where Is Up?. *269*
No, I'm Not William H. Macy *273*
Mommies Make the Best Dancers *275*

1

Back Home Down East

Jack Daniels Kept Me from Jim Beam and Johnnie Walker

Country Basketball

Cucumbers Remind Me of Stars and Lora

Gospel Music Led Me to Motorcycles

My English Teacher Was Strict and She Smoked Cigars

Oh Come to Me, My Sweet — Corn

Sometimes You Have to Leave to Find Yourself

A New Look at the Family

Jack Daniels Kept Me from Jim Beam and Johnnie Walker

The man handed the bottle of amber colored whiskey over to me.
"Here. Want some?" he said.
I was twelve years old.
It was 1965 and kids were telling Little Moron jokes, girls had cooties, ice trays had metal levers, the Beatles played Shea Stadium and Lyndon Johnson thought his Great Society needed more "oomph" so he signed Medicaid and Medicare into existence. Milk, not pizza, was delivered to your home and playing cowboys and Indians were loads of fun, not a cultural issue. Soda pop companies discovered they had a whole new group of customers — women — and so Tab, the soft drink, was beginning to show up in drink boxes — the refrigerated chest type that sat on the wooden porches of country stores.
Country stores with dirt parking lots, cars sitting on cinder blocks, trash burning in barrels, and Super A Farmall tractors were all part of life on our farm at Hudson's Crossroads or "the Crossroads" as it was called by cousins, uncles and everybody else that made a living there. It was acres and acres of work, frustration and joys all situated in the middle of the sandy farming soil of eastern North Carolina. It was the most beautiful and exciting place

in the world, though to look at it as you passed through on the paved, two lane state highway, it would appear to be just open land bordered with forests of pine trees and white blooming dogwood trees and the occasional house sitting a ways back off the road.

In the spring and summer, the Crossroads was surrounded by fields that bore green crops of tobacco and corn. In the mornings you could see a thin mist hide the tops of standing corn, where long and short eared beagles dashed across back roads chasing deer towards men waiting by their pickup trucks with rifles, where old folks dipped snuff and carried Dixie spit cups, where women sat in rockers on the front porch and hummed "Whispering Hope" and played with small children or shelled butterbeans, where people helped each other grade and pack golden flu cured tobacco as they worked all day sitting in "Pack Houses" — musty old barn like structures where the cured tobacco was stored until it was made ready to go to the warehouses in Greenville to be sold. It was a place where making a good biscuit was as important as your email account is today, and where women made boiled dinners of collards, fat back, sweet potatoes, and fried cornbread that was so good you savored each bite and thanked God for it.

Hudson's Crossroads was a place where your church attendance was as important as breathing and young men raced their Buicks, Fords and Chevrolets down dirt roads that threw up yellow dust, where the first hard frost meant hog killing and squirrel hunting, where kids would ride in the open back of a pickup truck while it bounced down a dirt road and your teeth jarred and your whole body would suddenly be thrown upward. The only nod to safety was your father telling you to "hang on and be careful." If you fell off it was your fault. On our farm a good grip was the first thing a kid needed to learn.

The farm was located about fifteen miles east of Greenville, which is about two hours east of Raleigh. Life moved constantly and meandered between lovely and nice and harsh and brutal. The farm could be a wonderful place to live at times when sweet corn was ready and gardens gave plenty but when the sky refused to give rain and the sun scorched everything bone dry then the farm had the temperament of a six foot cobra with strep throat.

Jack Daniels Kept Me from Jim Beam and Johnnie Walker

My father grew up at Hudson's Crossroads and my mother lived in Kinston until she met the man that would be my father, "Buddy," a red haired farm boy with slightly curly hair and a quick smile who loved to tap dance and tell a quick joke. He had served his time in the war and had come back home looking for work. While doing that he fell in love with my mother and they married.

At first they lived on the farm with my father's people in a house with a hand operated water pump, a tin roof, and a one-seat outhouse. They used five quilts on a bed in the winter where, according to my mother, when you were tired of looking up to see your breath you could look down between the floor boards and see the dogs under the house — and watch their breaths for awhile.

This was not the stereotypical genteel southern farm with men strolling about in white suits and shirts and southern belles wearing silk and satin like Scarlet O'Hara while they discussed new lace patterns and gossiped about who was sweet on who. Nobody I knew had servants or help that wore uniforms with white aprons or sat under a shade tree and strummed a banjo while singing about the Suwannee River. No, this was eastern North Carolina. Here men wore bib coveralls with brogans and women wore simple cotton dresses with pockets in the front for carrying matches, candy, yarn, or shotgun shells. You never knew what you might suddenly be required to do when raising children and livestock.

No mint juleps were ever served in our community that I knew of, but it was nothing to be wandering in the woods, as boys are apt to do sometimes, and come upon a whiskey still with the coiled copper worm and the big vats of boiling mash giving off an odor so sour it could make paint peel. You'd act like you never saw it, just keep looking straight ahead, maybe pick up your walking pace a bit, and as for the two men that were sitting on upturned drink crates with shotguns laid across their laps — what men?

People paid for their farms and houses and took care of their families by raising tobacco. It seemed to me that if ever there was a Jekyll and Hyde plant it was tobacco. It was cruel and fickle but it also fed and clothed all of us. Some men seemed to build altars to tobacco made of debt, barns, warehouses, and equipment, while others seemed to take it in stride and balanced their family and church life around it. The point was, tobacco touched everyone's life and you learned to help each other, to laugh at the good, and to accept the bad. Tobacco forced you to pull together. As long as your neighbor had a tractor, planter or sprayer, so did you.

Tobacco. Our lives ebbed and flowed according to the economic tides driven by that finicky, broad leaf, gummy, worm harboring, disease-infested weed. Tobacco demanded all your attention between May and September. Your morning started early, before the sun came up. A man had to figure out how best to make the life of a tobacco plant just a little bit better. Tobacco was insatiable for attention and demanded it be plowed at certain times in a particular way and that it be sprayed at certain stages with chemicals strong enough to kill a host of insects and fungi and life in galaxies far away. I've always blamed my inability to do math on being exposed to chemicals with names that contained more letters than Mississippi.

The tobacco had special needs like pulling, by hand one at a time, the small growths called suckers that sprang up between the leaf and the stalk. The sucker prevented nutrients from reaching the big broad leaves and would decrease the size and weight of the crop, which was a worry because cured tobacco was sold by weight. Each stalk of tobacco could have three or four suckers growing on it. For some reason, suckering tobacco seemed to be done only in 95 plus degree weather with humidity so thick it wrapped itself around you like a boa constrictor, sweat ran in your eyes, it stung, and made everything blur like a Monet painting. That invisible snake tightened itself around you and you fought for every breath. I don't know how many stalks of tobacco are in an acre, but after suckering acres and acres of tobacco for two or three weeks in a hot sun, day after day with only a Mason jar full of water to last you until lunch, you began to get a feeling for what Hell might be like and came to believe that the preacher at church knew exactly what he was talking about when he spoke of an eternal flame and an unquenchable thirst.

Tobacco pumped green hard cash into our homes, and in the 1960s and 70s, everything from food to school buildings, churches and highways were made possible by tobacco. Tobacco bought new trucks, nice Sunday clothes, braces for children's teeth, paid medical bills, put roofs on houses, purchased groceries, built bigger barns, and for the very lucky — wooden homes got bricked and concrete driveways got poured. Imagine — a concrete driveway — to drive on —and a dry place, free from the wind and dust, to park your car.

God, who watered our fields and gave us hope, wanted worship services held every Sunday morning at 10 o'clock sharp and so we did. We were Original Free Will Baptists, and we rode all the way to a small crossroads called Black Jack to attend church. The white board church was the center of most of our social activities.

The community prayed together and pulled together. When life threw a drought at us, or sickness seemed to be everywhere for a season, neighbors brought food to each other and fetched cool towels and brought a glass of water to a bedside.

During "The War" (Southern for the Civil War) our forebears had hidden Confederate soldiers from Yankee patrols and shared what little food they had with those fleeing the invading North. The church became a rallying point for the people and the community, and it still is up to this day. The church grew like a well-watered crop, and one day it became known as one of the largest rural churches in eastern North Carolina.

That's where we worshipped, at the Black Jack Original Free Will Baptist Church where the parking lot was dirt and men stood around outside dressed in their best pants and white shirts and gray fedora hats, smoking cigarettes in between services. Sometimes you'd see them bent over, white sleeves rolled up, looking under the hood of someone's car and using just a pocket knife or a dime for a screwdriver and make some adjustment so a person could get back home after service was over.

When Sunday school was over you filed into the main sanctuary and claimed a seat, hopefully a place underneath one of the oscillating General Electric fans mounted on the walls about head high. Those fans bathed you in hot air and like mythical sirens their gentle humming threatened to dash consciousness against the rocks and lull you into a nap after the first five minutes of a sermon. In addition, each pew had several wooden handle cardboard fans from the S.G. Wilkerson and Sons Funeral Home that had pictures on them of Jesus holding a lamb or Moses carrying the tablets of the

Ten Commandments while looking up to God like he was going to ask God a question.

The gospel was pumped out from our little white board church to spiritually irrigate the whole community, to saturate it in hope and grace, and to heed the hymn that said

"Work, when the day grows brighter,
Work in the noonday sun.
Work for the night is coming,
When man's work is done."

Everybody worked all day long, hard and fast, like night was just around the corner.

Men with cigarettes dangling from the sides of their mouths plowed, hoed, cussed, spit, hollered, bled, laughed and prayed trying to do anything they could to coax a healthy crop of tobacco or corn out of the ground only to see it burn up in the fields during a drought or turn yellow and wilt from too much rain. Storms brought hail and destroyed the crop or blew down the barns leaving only twisted tin and scattered wood. Women and children walked the fields replacing the tobacco that had died with fresh, green, healthy plants. The work aged men before their time, and mules that pulled tobacco trucks in the field got sick from the heat and would hang their huge heads and refuse to move. You could hit a mule and you could yell at it all you wanted but the truth of the matter was the mules didn't care about prosperity. Mules didn't want bigger barns or brick houses, they just wanted shade.

Tobacco did not recognize race. It hated everybody with such a vengeance and tenacity that it took white and black to make a harvest, and you did it stalk by stalk, picking one leaf at a time by hand. Once you got an armful you carried the leaves to a waiting tobacco truck that had sides made of old burlap bags all mounted on one axle and a frame with two used rubber tires all pulled by a mule or tractor. When the truck was full it was transported out of the field and to the shelter, which could be miles away. Once the leaves were at the shelter, women, both white and black, took the tobacco out of the truck and tied it to what we called "tobacco sticks," which in turn would be hung up later in a barn and cured. It was hard labor every step of the way. Everybody got a chance to laugh, sweat, cuss, and bleed.

At the end of the day, when the barn was full and the door closed, soft voices, tired from labor would manage to laugh about some little thing that happened and before long everyone was telling funny stories about the day. There was backslapping, grins, and a sense of togetherness. To fill a barn up with heavy green tobacco called for teamwork so everybody worked together which was as natural to us as breathing.

White and black both worried about debts, shoes, and shelter and getting the tobacco into the barn. While most of the blacks I knew were tenants they were regarded more as neighbors. When you work beside a man in a hot field you both sweat, you both get thirsty, and you both wish you were somewhere else.

While tobacco drew hard lines of demand, there were some soft edges to life. Some of the best times came by way of the homecomings or dinners on the grounds held at church during September or October. Dinner on the grounds was something you looked forward to and everyone brought a special dish — maybe potato salad, fried chicken, preserves, deviled eggs, sweet potato casseroles, baked ham, green beans, okra in vinegar along with tomatoes and pies and cakes. You drank sweet ice tea, and for a while, you forgot about the fields and the hogs and the power tobacco had over your life and people rested and gossiped and enjoyed each other's company. You sort of wonder if this wasn't the way the seventh day went for God, what with the angels to talk to and the wonders He had made.

The aches and pains were sometimes eased by Gospel sings that were held every fifth Sunday night where you could hear the promises of the Bible put to music and just imagine what your new body would look like and how it would feel to know sorrow and sickness no more. You thought about all this while babies crawled along the pews or were picked up by patient loving women and bounced on knees while the piano played "When the Roll is Called Up Yonder." You sang it loud with confidence, hardly needing to look at the green Broadman Hymnal because you knew the words by heart. After the opening songs there might be prayer requests made and you'd bow your head but sometimes you kept your eyes open and watched the girls your age who seemed to be getting new heavenly bodies kind of early. You'd suddenly find yourself, in your own way, praying for them too.

Family reunions also took the bitterness out of farming as the women would fry chicken or the men might barbeque a hog. While the food cooked, men would gather under a tree, smoke cigarettes and squat or sit on anything handy. Unlike today's parents, ours did not sit around and discuss the best schools or which teacher was good or bad and describe in minute detail every move and word their kids had achieved in the last week. The adults raised children to know manners and a child did not get praise unless he or she earned it. Not one kid that I grew up with ever needed therapy then or later because a nearby hickory switch helped clear up all issues, immediately. In those days, "inner feelings" were associated with a good bowel movement.

A child did not give an adult his take on life but instead children were told to go somewhere and play and not bother folks while the adults discussed the Democrats, aphids, gas mileage or the best piece of land for planting next year's crop. And no matter what they started off talking about be it politics, weather or hog feed, it always came back to tobacco.

So it was in this backdrop of whispering pines, sandy soil, tobacco and religion that I came along. I was born in 1953 and by the time I reached twelve, I was seeing an age die and a new one being born. I got to watch old ways get weak, stagger, gasp, and die as the woods were cut to make way for subdivisions, dirt roads were covered with asphalt, and the drink chests were replaced with coin operated machines. Our black and white Philco TV showed scenes of people in Montgomery, Alabama demonstrating around a courthouse and police came out with horses and night sticks and tried but failed to keep things the way they had always been.

The new age was born in fire, with cities burning so people could have the right to vote, and schools were integrated by force and tear gas. The South began to get people with northern accents. Pick-up trucks began sporting chrome wheels and dual exhausts and the blacks and whites fell into a new relationship that neither party was sure about, but they all started eating in restaurants together and using the same restrooms.

Now homes not only had concrete driveways but garages, cotton dresses gave way to polyester suits and skirts and ladies began to have hair appointments. There was no longer a need to use a pocketknife to adjust a carburetor because one of the several local garages did that now and mules were being replaced with big John Deere tractors while machines made tobacco easier to harvest. In the city they had something called "pizza delivery."

There were hunting clubs with land that allowed only members to hunt on it and transistor radios let you listen to music almost anywhere like in a tobacco field, parking lot, or your bedroom at night. The schools got bigger and the roads got wider.

Our church continued to grow and we made a nursery to contain the small children during the church service and a sound system was installed and people began to sing the songs that were featured on *The Gospel Jubilee* TV show. The old GE electric fans beside the stained glass windows gave way to central air conditioning and hymnals went from green to red with gold lettering on the front.

And tobacco continued to pay for it all.

. . .

No one liked farming tobacco but when it came to harvesting tobacco I had the best job of all. I was a "trucker." Mules had become scarce and everybody had one, if not two tractors of different sizes.

A "trucker" drove a tractor from the fields to the barns pulling tobacco trucks loaded with big green tobacco leaves. Truckers hung out with the "primers" — men in the field who pulled each leaf of tobacco from the stalk by hand. As a farm boy, I spent most of my summers with these men who, to pass the long hot hours of tedious work, discussed at great length the subjects of sex and drinking.

By the time I was twelve years old, there was nothing I had not heard about human reproduction, the organs involved, and the whiskey and wine that seemed to go with it. Our primers were black tenants and laborers that worked hard and tried to live even harder. Payday meant a trip to the city where whiskey and wine was bought and quickly consumed.

One might think that they wasted their wages but to hear them tell their stories, a young curious adolescent boy would think it was money well spent. I had seen some *Playboy* pin up pictures, but *Playboy* was small potatoes to these experts. Sex was always the topic of the day as the men would recount their adventures the week before. Seemed to me there was a lot to look forward to in life.

The second best thing to sex, from listening to the stories, seemed to be drinking, lots of it, for days at a time if you had the money. A lot of bragging went on as to who could drink the most and many a story was told as to what happened once one of them was thoroughly sauced. I spent days and years with these men and admired them for their work and humor. We smoked cigarettes together and discussed the best ways to catch perch and catfish.

Seemed no matter if they won or lost a fight, got caught with another man's wife or awoke to find all their money gone, they still laughed about it and they took for granted that the sun would come up the next day because it always did — and they always worked.

One man lived as a tenant on my uncle's farm but worked for us at various times. We had a lot of the same likes and dislikes, he laughed at my jokes, knew the best creeks for fishing, and taught me about crops and how to get a Farmall tractor to go faster.

He was a tall muscular, bald headed black man we called Jack Daniels — just like the whiskey — and everyone kidded him about his name. Jack lived with his wife, Skeeter, a slim, quick tempered woman and they drank, fought, laughed, went to jail, got out of jail, smoked Camel cigarettes, and treated me like family. Jack loved to pull your leg about something by spinning some long story. Then he'd grin a big wide white toothed grin so you knew he was lying, and it was always a funny lie, the kind of lie that used enough truth to make you realize he was making a point about something and just enough humor to make you laugh.

He was paid like everybody else, just enough to keep skin and bone together — rarely kept the electric bill paid for the three hanging light bulbs in the house. Jack never could afford to buy his namesake drink so instead he bought cheap liquor every payday.

Jack Daniels Kept Me from Jim Beam and Johnnie Walker

Jack didn't treat me like a kid — he made me work like a man. When we topped and suckered tobacco, Jack set the pace with no mercy and he'd tease you if you fell behind. Jack showed me how to run my hand down a tobacco stalk so you could tear the suckers out in about two moves and then you went to the next stalk and you did this for hours on end. He taught me how to watch for snakes that liked to wrap around tobacco stalks in the early mornings, and how to decide which side of a field to start on so the sun was mostly at your back during the day.

I followed Jack around the farm like a puppy and he taught me to shoot a .22 rifle before I was supposed to, gave me cigarettes, and taught me to change the thermostat in the Farmall. By eleven years of age, with his help and a lot of practice, I could blow perfect smoke rings and adjust the timing on anything that had cylinders.

Jack seemed to know everything like which days would be good for squirrel hunting, the best way to fry up a rabbit, which pond the fish were biting in, why the tractor wouldn't start, which clouds would make a storm and which clouds you didn't have to worry about. Jack had seen a copperhead snake bite a man's arm one time and he helped the man tie a tourniquet — a big deal and an amazing story to a white boy who had only played with frogs and turtles. Jack could fix anything that had gas, oil and tires — maybe not permanently but he could get you out of the field and back to the house. He knew everything except how to stay away from that liquid fire that seem to bring him peace for a little while and gave him something to look forward to so that life was a bit easier with a warm feel to it.

And so we all worked in the tobacco field, which in July was fit only for devils and flies. The days were so hot birds wouldn't even fly, but there we were working in sandy soil that seemed to burn through the soles of your shoes. Time goes by slow in a hot field and every move takes all your strength and the sweat clings to your body as though the Devil was trying to baste your soul. You breathed with your nose flared and your mouth open, but the air was so hot it brought no more relief than if you inhaled hot car exhaust. My father brought ice water in two or three mason jars and we all drank out of it, taking big swallows and passing it around to each other.

Big Decisions Are Best Made with Hotdogs

We never gave a thought about white and black drinking out of the same jar. Real thirst has no respect for race or color.

But there was always a back up to make things go a bit easier. The primers always somehow manage to bring red wine or liquor to the field without my father knowing it. Those are drinks that don't need ice to bring relief.

On one particular day we were harvesting tobacco and things seemed to drag along more slowly than usual. The heat was unreal. The sun threw everything it had at us, x-rays, violet rays, gamma rays — any rays it could hurl at us. Or maybe we'd somehow gotten under God's magnifying glass and He'd zeroed all the heat in the world down on us. For some reason on this particular day no one had brought water to the field, and I'd never been so thirsty. Everybody was going crazy with thirst. We had even walked over to a small ditch with slow moving black water in it hoping to see some that was fit to drink. The ditch flowed downstream from our hog pen so we knew we shouldn't drink it but our throats ached, and our tongues were beginning to feel swollen. We decided to not drink it but the black slimy water did look cool and so refreshing. I remember sticking my hand in the ditch just to feel something cool and being disappointed to discover that even the water in the ditch was warm and left a stain on your skin.

Crazy with thirst and with a need to get out of the hot sun for a bit, we walked over to a huge oak tree that grew at one end of the field and sat down. Jack reached over, his big biceps and back muscles rippling from the effort, and picked up the shirt he'd taken off hours ago. When he turned around he was grinning and holding a full pint bottle of liquor. The other primers, Mook, Nub, and Jake, started grinning and hooting. To me it looked like ice tea, and I could just imagine cold sweet tea running across my tongue and down my throat.

Jack took a drink and passed the bottle around. In the field everyone shared mason jars of water so it just seemed natural when Jack offered me a drink from the bottle. The white label on the bottle had a picture of a black crow walking across it, and the crow seemed to be enjoying himself.

"Here. Want some?" said Jack.

Jack Daniels Kept Me from Jim Beam and Johnnie Walker

So there I was, twelve years old and going crazy with thirst. I took the bottle from his hand.

I still had ice tea on my mind. When you're really thirsty the mind begins to make things seem the way you'd really want it to be. A warm breeze can actually be considered somewhat cooling and you can close your eyes and lick the sweat off your dry lips and for a moment they actually feel wet and refreshed. Put the mind under enough heat and it can imagine anything. I knew what Jack was offering wasn't tea, but it looked like tea, it was wet like tea, and I wanted something cold and wet so bad that I could, well, I could taste it — could almost feel the coolness in my mouth.

I lifted the bottle to my lips and drank it like you would iced tea — one long deep pull on the bottle, swallowed it and at first felt a wonderful liquid in my mouth, a bit warm but I couldn't help it, some reflex took over and I took another big mouthful. My mouth was so full that my cheeks puffed out and I forced myself to swallow it all.

I waited for that refreshed feeling, the feeling your mouth gets when it's finally been relieved of that dry aching feeling that makes you desperate for something to drink.

But my brain was puzzled. Where was the coolness I had anticipated, and where was the tea taste? Something was very wrong. My mouth was tingling, becoming warm, growing hot, now burning.

I saw Jack step towards me — in what seemed to be slow motion — and he yelled "No! Not like that Joey! Just a little bit!"

But it was too late. Oh honey, it was oh, so too late.

My eyes crossed then watered up. My throat was one long tube of pure fire! I couldn't breathe! I dropped the bottle, saw the black crow hit the ground, and went to my hands and knees trying to find fresh air — had to be some somewhere. God had made this great big round green earth and surrounded it with air and I couldn't find any of it.

I suddenly knew why preachers said don't drink liquor — don't even look at it. I had gone to Hell from the inside out! I saw small points of light and wondered if my brain had exploded.

I looked down, got dizzy and saw tiny specs of sand rising up to my face. Air! Good Lord, where was the air? I'd had plenty of it just a while ago! My mouth tasted like I had a dead badger in it and my tongue and stomach were burning like a brush fire. I was shaking, trying to heave everything out but nothing would come up, just that infernal horrible fire raging in my gut. I opened my mouth wide to try and say something but my throat was hot and constricted, no sound would come out. I looked like a fish trying to breathe. Water was pouring out of my eyes and snot running out of my nose.

I heard the other primers start heehawing and falling all over themselves laughing, and I realized Jack was pounding me on the back but laughing so hard he could hardly get his words out.

"It'll b-be alright Joey b-b-boy. Y-y-you drank n-n-near half the b-b-bottle!" Jack was laughing and giggling so hard he had fallen to the ground on his knees beside me. "J-j-just breathe, damn boy, just b-b-breathe!" He fell over in the dirt and howled. The ground beneath me turned, all of it, and then I saw the blue sky.

I thought, so this is what dying is like.

The clouds seemed so calm up there, like they were trying to reassure me this was all right, that this is how you die, just lie back and let the fire take you.

Time seemed suspended while a raging fire blazed in my stomach and throat. Then wonderfully, within about two minutes my breathing became steady, the burning subsided and life seemed to be just, well, better. I remember getting on my hands and knees and staring at the dirt for a while.

They said that once I got my legs back under me and returned to the field that I was the happiest trucking kiddo they'd seen in years. My driving the tractor seemed to consist of weaving and quick braking with false starts but I didn't care. In fact there was a lot now I didn't care about anymore like what really happened to the dinosaurs, the mystery of sex and the concept of America. Instead, I felt like singing — which I did. They said that for a white boy I did a pretty good version of "Mustang Sally" using an adjustable wrench for a microphone.

But liquor and the blazing hot sun do not mix and later that day the happiness, the euphoria and the songs turned on me like false friends and my head began to pound, my eyes ached and

Jack Daniels Kept Me from Jim Beam and Johnnie Walker

my stomach kept turning over and over. My head began to feel tight, an axe was buried in it just behind my eyes and I promised God that if the headache didn't kill me that I would never touch whiskey again. I promised all afternoon. And call me strange, but I decided I didn't like crows anymore either. It seemed to take years, but finally that day ended.

Obviously I lived — but just barely.

My relationship with tobacco went on for a few more seasons. Then I began dating girls and went to dances, and got a job in the city, learned to shave, and do Algebra, eat pizza and have an opinion about politics. I lost interest in fishing, blowing smoke rings, changing thermostats in tractors, and finding wild watermelons growing in the edge of the woods. I left the farm.

But I came home one day during tobacco season after I had been gone from the farm for a couple of years, and instead of tobacco trucks and primers, I saw a huge red machine that could go in a field and pick the tobacco. Now tobacco was simply crammed into a container, shoved inside a tunnel-like metal barn — there was no need for tobacco sticks anymore. Now there was no need for primers, truckers, or laborers. Jack and all those that were like him were gone. I never knew where Jack went or what became of him; nobody seemed to know though I asked around.

I learned a lot from Jack and the others but as time went by some of the things we laughed about and some of the things we did have grown dim in my mind, like paint on an old barn that fades and peels in the hot sun and only small weathered bits of it are left, not enough to be sure about the true color anymore.

High school and college are tempting years for a young man and though people tried me, men and women alike — I could never be tempted by liquor.

I was in the Atlanta airport some years ago waiting for a flight passing the time with two business associates. They ordered drinks, one a Jim Beam and the other a Johnnie Walker, both came straight with only ice cubes — looked just like tea. They offered to buy me a drink to celebrate our latest project and when I refused they began to insist in a good-natured kind of way, they were almost pleading. They suggested I have a shot of Jack Daniels if I didn't like what they were drinking. My flight was coming up soon and I grabbed my things, stood up and told them, "Boys, believe me. Jack Daniels taught me to stay away from Jim Beam and Johnnie Walker."

I smiled, and as I made my way through the crowd, I believe I heard Jack laughing all the way to the boarding gate.

Country Basketball

Jesus said to suffer the little children to come to him because Jesus knew about kids — he had been one himself. The little becomes the big and you should be careful how you treat a small person now because they become much bigger later in life.

And there was no better soil for growing little things into bigger things than on our farm. There are places in the world where you simply take up space and there are places you live and Hudson' Crossroads was about living, growing and making do with what you had. A kid learned to work hard, love bacon, and every once in a while he got to play.

Children were not coddled and pampered. If a kid wanted something you learned early to either imagine you had it, make it, or lie in the grass, look up into the sky and dream about it. Nobody was going to buy it for you.

The outdoors was our playground; you lived in it. Boys were treated like livestock, turned outside and left to wander and graze on their own. We peed behind trees and drank out of garden hoses. We were free range children, playing unsupervised, our imaginations were the only boundaries we knew and a kid could be and do about anything he wanted as long as you learned to work with what you had. Imagination was a wonderful thing to have in those days.

We could be spacemen on the moon, cowboys fighting desperate Indians or US army soldiers patrolling for German troops. We only had to imagine it. The yards, the fields, and the woods belonged to us. We could run free because we'd learned rules and how to behave — the world was not about us, we were no more special than anyone else — don't break in line, never interrupt and always wait your turn. We knew our place. It was an adult world and did not revolve around children, which takes a lot of stress off of a kid — we didn't need Ritalin or Zoloft. A kid did not give you his take on gay marriage or the Middle East situation, kids listened. The world favored grown-ups. Parents never had to explain things.

Many a question got a standard answer:
"Mom, I want a BB gun."
"No, go out and play."
"Why can't I have more drink (cola)?"
"Go out and play."
"Mom, I cut myself with my pocketknife." (A quick glance by the adult made sure you had all your fingers. The fact that you had a knife was irrelevant.)
"Go out and play."
"I can't find my baseball glove."
"Go out and play."
"I think the toilet's broke."
"Go out and play."

Just like that, no therapy, no concern about our inner feelings, no one cared or checked if the dirt was gluten free or if stones had been removed from the yard so that a fallen kid would not get cut, dirty, or bruised. Our yards were not filled with eight inches of sawdust to cushion a fall as you find in the engineered safety-oriented playgrounds today. You were expected to bleed — it happened. If, upon inspection, a bleeding wound showed no living bone then you were expected to get over it. Go out and play.

Outdoor sports brought us all together in those days but it depended on where you were and who you were with as to how it was played, something you could use later in life, especially if you went into politics. Kids had their own cultures and you learned to get along. One example was basketball.

Country Basketball

A lot of people don't know this but there are two kinds of basketball in the world — there is city basketball and there is country basketball.

City basketball is usually played in the center of civilization, amidst man's high buildings, paved roads, electric infrastructure, sodium lights, law and order, and respect for human life. It's nice.

City basketball is usually played on what is called a court. This court, like civilization, has order in the form of lines for boundaries and lines for foul shots. The court can be inside or outside, located on asphalt, concrete, or wood such as you find in a gymnasium with polished floors. City basketball is played in clean places or public buildings and it also has a "set of rules."

The goal of city basketball is to outscore your opponents, to rack up more goals by skillfully putting a basketball through a hoop, which is a metal rim with a net beneath it. You put the ball through the hoop more times than your opponent does. You do not hurt people intentionally in city basketball — it's against the rules.

One attempts to block an opponent's shots by waving their hands while jumping or crowding close, but not too close to the opposite player. And it's okay if you want to try and take the ball from your opponent as long as you follow the rules. Murder, mayhem, and cheating are forbidden.

But country basketball is different.

And country basketball was what I played.

We played it on hard packed dirt, dirt that had seen huge John Deere tractors roll over it carrying trailers full of tobacco or hogs. It was dirt that was blown in from the fields during the dry times and the rains came and packed it until it was like concrete with a fine gritty layer over it.

The boundaries for our "court" were always decided by the biggest kids. They pointed out imaginary lines between objects using whatever you had at hand — an old tree stump with an imaginary line, then to an engine block half buried in the dirt, then to a tree sapling growing just close enough to where you are playing, and then to maybe an old rusted paint can lying about in a suitable spot. And voila!, you had a country basketball court. Foul lines were decided on an as-need basis by the older kids with the player being advised to stand at a certain spot that was deemed "about right" for a foul shot.

Our rim was not metal nor did it have a net, but was often times a wooden bushel basket with the bottom rotted out. We'd find old rusty nails in the dirt, then find a hammer or a rock, and nail the basket to the side of the building or a tree that lent itself to the location of the court. A net was something we'd seen in books, but we never had one. That was for people in the city and on television.

The picking of teams was a disguised popularity contest, which was hard on a shy kid like me. You stood in a group while the leaders picked, each taking turns assessing your abilities in front of everyone, and then at some point your name was called. The order in which you were picked said a lot about your standing in the community and your skills as a player. I was usually next to last and was always looking off into the distance while the choosing took place as though this didn't mean much to me, like I had a flight out to Atlanta in thirty minutes or I'd just come back from climbing a volcano and was bushed. You tried to look bored but with initiative.

Finally this humiliating process ended and each team gathered together to plan strategy, which consisted of who would throw the ball in first. This was decided by a coin toss or the biggest, most muscular kid. From there we played by the seat of our pants.

Which was okay because the goal of country basketball is not to win as it is in city basketball. No, in country basketball the goal is to *survive*.

The ball was thrown and we'd begin moving about the court like a pack of hunting jackals looking for the weak, the hurt, searching for those that did not dribble fast enough.

During a game of country basketball a player may be taken out by any means available: tripping, biting, gouging, choking, kneeing, elbowing, landmines, bear traps, pistol whipping or grapeshot — it made no difference. The idea was to take the jerk out and score. This wasn't a game, it was a statement about who we were and what we were about. When we played country basketball we morphed into testosterone filled hunters and warriors.

So this was my life.

And it was a pretty darn good one to me. But life is funny and changes on little things; you really need to be careful.

On one particular day we'd just chosen our teams for a round of basketball. We were playing out behind my cousin's country store on packed dirt, the day was hot. When you perspired it did not come out in drops, but it ran in small rivulets down your nose and arms and into the dust, and the salt burned your eyes. It set the mood.

We were all burning under the sun, cursing under our breaths, and talking trash to each other as we bumped, jostled, and milled about like a herd of bunched up water buffalo waiting to cross a crocodile infested river. There were shouts and yelps as someone received an elbow to their kidneys or a shoulder somehow plowed into someone's chest sending them reeling backward to bump into someone else which in turn all produced a steady stream of grunts and groans on the court. You would hear a big bellow every now and then when someone received a particularly painful blow to the back or shin. The action was fast, the ball moved from person to person, and the herd was following it.

Then, quite unexpectedly, I had the ball.

It was a fluke — wild luck on my part. An opponent, my cousin Randy, had thrown the ball to Gary who was knocked down from behind by Larry (our guy) and the ball whizzed past Gary and almost took me out with a direct hit to the nose. Sudden reflex on my part caused my hands to go up in self-defense and, voila! I had the ball.

I couldn't believe my luck. Not only did I have the ball but my teammates had already knocked everybody, and I mean every *body*, out of the way that stood between me and the goal (you could see people on the ground, hear a lot of groaning), and my guys had their arms stretched wide to prevent anyone from going around them thus forming an open path for me to approach the goal. It would be like running down an aisle.

I began dribbling the ball towards the goal picking up speed, I wanted to acquire some lift for the jump, and as I approached the goal everything was going just fine. I leaped bringing the ball up with my hands. I got good lift and thought for a moment that I might just make this a dunk shot. I rose higher towards the goal, my feet were off the ground and I was bringing the ball up for the shot when I felt a tug, like you feel when a big fish takes your line, the ball was slipping out of my hands and I realized what was happening. Crap!

Ronnie Everson.

Ronnie, a year older than me and the shortest guy in the community, was hated on a basketball court. He was always one of the first to be picked for a team, not because he was any good, but because of one trait he had that an opponent despised. The boy could steal a ball.

His blond hair was worn in a crew cut; he had slightly bucked front teeth and always appeared where he was least wanted. He ran like a short little crab — sort of sideways with his hands acting like crab pinchers — always moving, reaching towards the ball, trying to slap it out of your hands or grab it and pass it on to a team mate.

Ronnie was good at stealing the ball, and he was hated for it. He rarely ever shot. He was so short you could place your hand on the top of his head and hold him there long enough to pound the ball out of his hands, so he'd learned to pass the ball quickly.

Another thing, you never left Ronnie on his feet. You always tripped him when you could. If you left him standing he'd come back and take you out from behind at the knees. No, you never left Ronnie standing.

I remember the horror as I realized that my hands were now empty, hands without a basketball, hands that were now void of anything that mattered. They may as well have been amputated.

I screamed "*No!*" The shot was lost, dreams of glory, and a new elevated place in the world of my peers were gone. All gone.

That's when, while still in the air empty handed, I looked down and saw Ronnie had broken the most basic rule of country basketball. He was standing still. Never stand still while you're playing country basketball, you become a target and somebody will take you out. No kidding. It's legal.

I came down and bent my arm so my elbow was aimed directly at his little head, right on the bridge of his nose, and when I connected it was over quick. Whap! Ronnie went down like a sack of seed.

He screamed, his hands clawed at this face while he rolled on the ground in pain with dust and dirt mixing with blood and snot. He writhed, moaned, balled up like a fetus, opened his mouth to breath and took in dirt which in turn made him cough and yell and cry all at the same time. We thought he might be hurt.

We stopped the game long enough to find a pulse. Then we dumped his body under a nearby tree.

The game was a good one. I got in a couple of long shots, took a hit to the ribs from Randy but gave it back later with an accidental elbow to his gut. We went on to lose 16 to 12 and with it, my one chance to climb another rung of the ladder in the world of kid prominence and glory.

The last I saw of Ronnie, he was limping towards his brother's car, his face smudged with dirt and blood and tear streaks on his cheeks. Underneath the grime his one open eye (the other seemed swollen shut) glared at me as he walked by. He managed to give me a one finger salute as he got into his brother's car.

I didn't know it then but that would be the last time I would ever play basketball with little Ronnie. A short time after our game his family moved, his father decided to give up farming and find work in Raleigh. Meanwhile back on the farm we did our chores, we played our games and life went on.

I liked the next phase of life a lot. It had girls in it. I would go on to explore the wonder of the first crush. She was a beautiful girl with long flowing brown hair and according to our preacher one day we would all get heavenly bodies but I felt this girl had already gotten hers. We were taught to pray for each other in the Black Jack Original Free Will Baptist Church where she and I attended, it was a Christian's duty. I prayed for her night and day.

But we all know first love is usually just a speed bump in life. You hit it quite unexpectedly, we rattle, our inner suspension heaves and strains and then we're over it, and we go on to other loves and experiences.

I spent the next few years being quite active in our church and working odd jobs while going to school and by the time I was twenty three years old, I was teaching a youth class at our church. I attended a college night class at this time and on this particular night, needed to end a Bible study class early in order to get to Greenville, twenty miles away and take an important exam.

I said "Amen," dismissed the class and ran to my car. It was normally a twenty-five minute drive to Greenville, I was determined to make it in fifteen.

I took a back country road that would be a short cut and opened up all eight cylinders of my two door Pontiac Firebird. I had just made the first two payments. The car was doing beautifully, hugging curves, sitting low in the straights and the pine trees on both sides of the road were becoming blurs.

As I gained more speed the road seemed to narrow and form a small "V", the needle was showing ninety miles an hour and climbing when the car suddenly filled with a strange light I'd never seen before. A quick check in the rear view mirror revealed a twirling blue light, the kind that is mounted on the car of every North Carolina Highway Patrol vehicle. Not good. I decelerated and pulled over to the shoulder, the wheels made small bumping sounds on the dirt. The trooper pulled in behind me.

In the side view mirror I saw the tall trooper, outlined by his headlights, walk slowly up to my vehicle. I rolled down my window.

"Afternoon officer," I smiled.

"Afternoon. May I see your license?"

"Got'em right here." I beamed my best smile at him, fumbled to get my wallet out of my pocket and hand him the driver's license — with another big beaming smile.

He had a flashlight that could double as a nightstick and brought the license up closer in the light. He stared at it for a moment.

Then he said in voice that had a ring to it, "Well, well, hello Joe Hudson!"

I looked up, squinted, tried to make out features and put the voice together. The big tall man wearing a gun with the full force of the law was looking down on me and smiling. Oh, God. It couldn't be.

Little Ronnie Everson had grown up and was now a North Carolina State Highway Patrolman! I pegged him to be about 6 feet tall — and wearing a gun.

Any hopes of using old times to avoid a citation were dashed when Ronnie flipped his ticket book open, took out his pen, bent down low to my window so he could see my eyes and said, "Played any basketball lately?"

I swear he sounded nasal.

The little had become the big.

I accepted the ticket with resignation and a weak smile. After all, given the rules of country basketball, this was a perfectly legal move.

Cucumbers Remind Me of Stars and Lora

When I was fourteen years old my father informed me that my uncle Larry needed help on a cucumber grader that Larry owned. According to my father I could make some extra money and still help him (Dad) on our farm. Before I could speak my father said, "I'll tell Larry you'll be there tomorrow." Oh. Joy. When I reported for work I found my cousin Randy and two other buddies had been pressed into service. This was before kids had lawyers.

Working on a cucumber grader in eastern North Carolina during the summer was equivalent to working the salt mines of the Roman Empire only the Romans treated their slaves a bit better. In Rome you got to die.

The cucumber grader is a machine set under a large tin roofed shelter big enough to allow trucks to back in and unload bags of cucumbers (cukes). The machine itself is about fifteen feet long and shakes the cukes into different slots according to their size and dumps them into bushel baskets. The laborer (me) removes a full basket, about sixty pounds, and lifts it onto a scale. The basket is weighed by someone who sat in a chair and made more money than I did. I was paid twenty-five cents an hour for this in 100-degree heat. The grader opened at 6 a.m. and closed when Uncle Larry said so, usually about 9 o'clock at night.

One evening my uncle announced that a truck would arrive just after midnight to take away the cukes for that day. The truck must be loaded upon arrival so we would stay all night and not go home. He had spoken to our parents, told them not worry, that we could sleep anywhere at the shelter and no, blankets would not be needed, the temperature had not fallen below 90 degrees for the past three nights. The boys would be fine. Child care was different in those days.

We finished loading the truck around 3 a.m., and all the adults went home. The night was humid and hot and us boys climbed up onto the tin roof and lay down. Randy had found a pack of Winston cigarettes, and we smoked them while we lay on our backs under God's Big Night Blanket. For a while we practiced blowing smoke rings. We practiced tapping the side of our mouths just as you blow the smoke out, makes a nice ring. There were just a few cigarettes in the pack, and we went through them pretty quick and so we laid back and became still on the cool tin roof.

The night sky was clear and huge and we laid there, hands clasped behind our heads, looking at billions of stars and it made us feel very small.

There were no soft beds out there in that universe — no TV shows, no baseball games, no US Constitution, no Superman comic books, or chewing gum. We felt so insignificant — little itty bitty us looking up at the Great Unknown. The Big Dipper looked as though it was inches from my face, like I could reach out and touch it if I wanted to.

We all felt the wonder of that night sky but did not know how to express ourselves so we said things that boys would normally think were dumb. "It's beautiful ain't it?" (dumb) and "Makes you feel small don't it?" (real dumb). A string of stars went off to the left starting from my right foot, and I wondered if Red Hudson, an ancestor of mine that fought in the War Between the States, had seen those same stars. I wondered if he had smoked. I wondered what it was like to walk on the moon. I wondered what would ever become of me. I wondered if I was handsome or ugly. I wondered what it was like to kiss a girl.

I stared at those stars and thought about a girl I liked, Lora. She had brown eyes and one time at school by accident I touched her hair as she walked by me. I liked her voice and she had a way of smiling that made me feel good, made me feel a need to talk to her, to just be around her. For reasons I didn't understand, I wanted her to be safe, to be happy, to think I was cool. I laid there on that roof and thought about her for hours until a reddish streak appeared low on the horizon and it was morning. We climbed down from the roof; we had a lot of work to do.

Sometimes when I smell the tangy clean smell of fresh cucumbers or stand beneath a big summer night sky I think about that night and those stars. I never told Lora how I felt or ever got to know her well. But still, I hope she's all right.

Gospel Music Led Me to Motorcycles

I like to listen to southern gospel music — The Happy Goodman Family, The Cathedrals, The Gaithers, etc. Most people listen to it and think about Heaven, God and spiritual things. Me, I think motorcycles.

For almost twelve years I traveled and played with a gospel singing group called The Melody Makers. I've played in every kind of church for about every kind of crowd there is — the upscale ones, the formal ones, and the crowd that brings reptiles to church.

I was about eighteen years old when one night the group was playing in an extremely "rustic" church off the main roads. Right in the middle of a song, a "brother" pulled out what appeared at first to be a brown rope, or a brown snake, or a power cord. I really didn't want to know.

Fortunately the show ended after that song, and I became leader of the group. I led — right off the stage, out the door, across the parking lot, and to the van. As I ran through the parking lot I discussed the snake thing with the Lord. We both agreed to keep what I said between friends.

Later that week we played to a large crowd in an auditorium. We had been on the road for several nights and I was looking forward to packing up and getting back home. That's when my life took a turn.

We were informed by our bass singer and leader, Donnie, that a deal had been made and we were going to be cutting an album in Madison, Kentucky. The producer was going to be none other than Rusty Goodman.

Now in case you don't know, the Happy Goodman Family in the 1960s-80s was to gospel music what the Beatles were to pop music.

Part of the experience involved us opening a show for the Goodman Family and we got to meet Rusty. I went giggly and stuttered as we all took turns introducing ourselves to him. Long story short, the show went great and I was awed that Rusty Goodman— the greatest gospel music composer of all times — was going to produce our album in the Goodman studio.

At the appointed day and time the group was at the studio waiting for The Man to arrive. I'll never forget standing in the same room where gospel classics had been recorded like "I Wouldn't Take Nothing for My Journey Now" and "Who Am I?" I kept looking for Rusty to enter the studio. It would not have surprised me if he had descended through the roof with bright white lights while angels and cherubim's announced his coming. The guy was an icon to us. But instead of a divine like entrance I heard a click, the door opened and there he was — in black leather riding chaps, a black Harley jacket, helmet and black riding boots! What the...? I fell in love with Christianity all over again.

There he stood, the great Rusty Goodman. He had bushy hair and a big wide grin plastered all over his face. He gave us a warm strong handshake and immediately made us feel at home.

Donnie had to ask him....what was with the motorcycle get up? Somehow we expected him to walk in holding a microphone dressed in a suit, as though he was on stage. Rusty laughed. Turns out he had just bought a big Harley Davidson "hawg" and was in love with motorcycle riding.

He told us what it was like to ride his Harley — the rush of wind in your face, the smell of trees and flowers all around you as you ride down the road with the asphalt only inches from your feet. While he was talking, a studio engineer began to shoo everyone towards the sound booths, time was money. Everyone else moved into the studio but I stayed behind, asking Rusty about his bike and hanging on to every word. He must have seen that look in my eyes, the look a person gets when they've come to realize there is something new in life and they'd like to try it. When we took our first break from recording that day he motioned me outside.

Rusty let me sit on his Harley "hawg," and the great icon of gospel music explained to me how a motorcycle worked and why it may be the choice of transportation in Heaven. He took me for a ride, and when I came back I decided two things: (1) If motorcycles were good enough for Rusty Goodman, they were good enough for me. (2) Get one.

No one ever performs songs for kids at gospel sings so I had been writing children's songs to add to our show. I played one for Rusty and he thought it was great. It was about a pet frog that gets killed by a truck and goes to Heaven. Looking back, it wasn't a very good song but Rusty encouraged me to keep at it and I did. I would go on to write a Christian family program called *The Front Porch,* which ran in our church for about five years.

How blessed I was to meet someone so famous yet kind to a dumb kid and by sharing and giving words of encouragement, influenced the direction of a life. Rusty died in 1990.

Now, whenever people sing southern gospel I hear the potato-potato-potato sound of a Harley from long ago, I smell black leather, and hear a kind voice.

I would write more about how we got to know the Goodman family a bit, how we went on to cut another album with Rusty, but it's a beautiful day outside and I seem to hear a kind voice telling me to drop everything — go for a ride on my motorcycle. So I'm going to do it and I'll probably sing some songs, some old songs that go with memories. Catch you later.

My English Teacher Was Strict and She Smoked Cigars

The house I live in was constructed as a tri-level home in 1976. Tri-level homes were invented by Nazi architects. You must constantly go up and down stairs in order to access different rooms. In addition, the Gestapo ordered a counter with an overhanging cabinet in our kitchen. It's a convenient counter as our mail, pocketbooks, scraps of paper, basket of fruit, newspapers, small babies, car keys — all seem to collect on this counter. However if you become engrossed looking at an item and lean over, BAM, your head slams into the overhead cabinet. I do this about 237 times a year, and we've been living in the house now for about twenty years. My vocabulary and memory are both decreasing.

One day I hit the cabinet hard and heard a snort and giggle as my little boy was behind me. He thought it was hilarious to see daddy bang his head on a large, ever-present, nonmoving kitchen cabinet. Right then my vocabulary actually increased, but I managed to reel in most of the nouns.

"Do again, Daddy, do again!" my son pleaded. He looked blurry and sounded far away.

Big Decisions Are Best Made with Hotdogs

As little black and white birds flew in circles around my head I realized that, (1) the world will not step out of your way so be very careful, (2) in a society that encourages individuality, has fifty free states and hundreds of cable channels, it is good we have common universal experiences (BAM — ouch!), and (3) something about pain, but now I forget.

The bump was pretty bad and reminded me of my high school Journalism/English teacher, Miss Ann Nelson. She was a smart, quick witted, short ball of fire who wore black horn rimmed glasses and bright red lipstick. I observed her one day outside in the smoking area and while the other teachers smoked their Pal Malls, Winston and Camel cigarettes, Miss Nelson was blowing out blue smoke from a cigar. I thought that was so cool. She also had a small bump on her forehead that only became apparent when she leaned over your desk and handed you a paper marked "needs improvement."

We like to think that teachers nourish (You Can Be The President, Follow Your Heart, Dream Big), but Miss Nelson demanded perfect spelling and proper grammar like a marine drill instructor demands pushups. The woman would have eaten any Child Left Behind — it would have been her punch line to a joke. She hated political B.S.

If you misspelled more than one word in a story you got an automatic "D" which I thought was unreasonable. Suppose a story was actually "A" material? According to Miss Nelson, Webster made a fine dictionary — use it or suffer, kiddo.

One day she marked my paper a "C." In the margin she had written notes like "What do you mean?" and "Awkward sentence" and "Oh Good Grief!" I challenged her. The class had voted my story as the very best. She was not being fair and I wanted to know — what was the problem? She glared at me over her glasses and said, "You have ability. I grade you on a higher bar. Quit whining and write." And I did.

She became my favorite teacher and introduced me to the *New York Times* and William Sidney Porter. The day I graduated high school she gave me a book of quotations from famous authors. I still have it. I saw her some years before she passed away. At that time I was writing a Christian family show and had sold a short story to a magazine in California. I told her all about it and she was so proud.

I think about her every week when I write my column and also whenever I bump my head. She would like that.

Oh Come to Me, My Sweet — Corn

I was born in January, a cold dark month. I arrived totally disoriented and without any clothes, was hoisted up by my feet, given a good whack, and thus welcomed into the world. The mood in the room was somber, people avoided looking at each other. No one wanted to say anything that was depressing. It was like there was an elephant in the room but no one wanted to call attention to it. Hearts were heavy. The doctor, nurses and my parents all knew the sad truth — I had missed the sweet corn season by six months.

Just mention the corn year of '53 and older people in my community get dreamy, become trancelike, and they drool. Corn connoisseurs say the crop that year was especially vibrant, a wonderful bouquet of earthy tartness balanced by the sweetness of the sugar with delicate hints of fried bacon. It was said that a farmer in the community, so enthused about the new crop, ate twenty ears of cooked corn in one sitting and then, so caught up in the wonderful taste of those yellow kernels, he then made and ate a corn pudding casserole and (alas!) lost his taste for corn. He sold the farm and played sad songs on a harmonica. He never got over it.

From the time I was a small child, corn has always been a source of wonder and delight. We grew the corn close to the house, and when it was "ready" my mother would march our family into the field at sunrise where we picked corn by hand and put in it in bushel baskets. Then we brought it back to the house, sat in the shade of a huge oak tree, and there we would shuck, silk, and stack the corn like gold bars. The bigger my pile grew so did my glory. "Oh my," Mother would say. "You're such a hard worker! Look! Look everybody!" This produced frowns from my sisters but I'd smile at them and try to remain humble. God favored people like me.

Later work moved into the kitchen which became a boiler room filled with clouds of steam from the pressure cooker and pots full of boiling water for sterilizing the jars — all of which had the name "Ball" written on them in cursive writing. We washed the corn in the kitchen sink passing the ears to my mother who slaved away at the canning process, her damp hair stuck to her forehead as if she'd just stepped out of the shower.

Mother would boil us fresh ears of corn for lunch, and we'd sit outside on the ground and eat it like beavers. No juice was ever so sweet and no crunch so tender as sweet corn cooked, salted, and buttered by your mother.

Corn is the grain of America. From it came a TV show set in a cornfield. A generation grew up watching *Hee Haw* with Junior Samples who gave out the most famous telephone number in the world — "BR-549."

Corn mash is used to make whisky, which is the foundation of the Kennedy family's wealth and without them there would have been no news to report in the 1960s and 70s. There would have been no need for Walter Cronkite or the word "Chappaquiddick."

Without corn chips how would we eat salsa? With a spoon? Yucko, amigo.

Now corn stands accused of giving us unhealthy love handles that hang over our belts. Corn syrup is the least health giving and the most fattening of the carbon consuming foods.

Ethanol, a mash that is one part corn and two parts tax dollars, consumes about as much energy as it yields.

Corn is another tradition the health police are trying to take away from us. But I say to corn, come hither "Golden Jubilee," come to me my "Silver Queen." We go back a ways. Today it seems anything that you enjoy is bad for you. I can remember when sunshine and fresh air were considered good for you.

Now if you'll excuse me, I have some sweet corn to eat. With salt. And butter.

Sometimes You Have to Leave to Find Yourself

I grew up on a farm in eastern North Carolina, and one Friday night when I was nine years old, I walked past my father sitting in his recliner reading the newspaper. He spoke without putting the newspaper down and said, "We're going into hog business. Tomorrow." And just like that, my dreams of being an astronaut were put on hold.

We built pens, shelters and a farrowing house (the equivalent to a hog birthing and daycare center). I learned to pour concrete and dig post holes and do it all in ninety degree heat. Once that was done and all the electric fences were constructed, we filled the place up with hogs. I also learned that even if your cousin Randy dares you, never pee on a charged electric fence — you'll speak in tongues and flop around on the ground like a fish. When you get back up, you'll walk funny.

Now the idea of hog business is to make lots of little hogs (pigs), raise them up, sell them, complain about the low price of pork, grumble about the bank loan, and then do it all over again. My father was constantly going to the poor house in a new truck.

I gave names to some of my favorites — Porkchop, Oscar Mayer, and one particular lady hog I named Lou.

One day Lou put on some mascara and lip gloss, lit up a cigarette, and walked seductively by a group of men hogs. Most of those guys had an operation when they were young so they ignored Lou and just stood around sipping wine spritzers and discussing mutual funds. But one hog never had the operation, a 400 pound red Duroc boar who was propped against a fence post smoking a Pall Mall and when he saw Lou he said, "Hi, Good Looking" and they went off together to a cheap wire pen that charged by the hour and they didn't come out until late evening. My father explained that a miracle of life would come later.

And sure enough it did. A little over three months later, on a Saturday, the first wet sacks of life began to appear. My father and I watched the wonder of birth.

But as it turned out the wonder of birth was lost on Lou, she wasn't the maternal type. She seemed to regard her new family with disdain. She'd just lie there staring straight ahead while ten little squealing pigs used her as a milk hose. Later I'd come by to check on her, and she'd be pushing against the door with her snout. Lou wanted out of the deal. I remember one time when I'd checked to see that the gate was locked she looked at me with small accusing eyes as though to say, "One day, maybe a week, maybe a year, but one day I'm going to have a life. I'll go away and leave these little Wonders for you to take care of, Boss Man. See how you like it then."

I knew how she felt. Almost twenty-six years ago today, I bolted out the gate with a packed suitcase and never looked back. I headed west and stopped just short of the Smoky Mountains. I met people, made friends and put down roots which grew into a life. Sometimes you have to leave one place in order to find yourself in the next. Ever since moving to the city I've come to know exactly who I am. I'm a guy that wants to go back to the place he escaped from, the farm.

Sometimes I speak before a large crowds of people, most wearing business suits and ties, and everyone looks as though they wouldn't be caught dead doing manual labor. They will smile at me as though I am one of them, and at those times I want to scream "Guess what? I know how to drive a tractor. Ich bin ien Farm Boy!"

Sometimes You Have to Leave to Find Yourself

    Some days I stop the car, jump a ditch, stroll through open fields and gaze at livestock. I remember the farm, I miss it, and find it ironic that now I have days that I long to go back to the place I escaped. I like to stand in a field and smell the dirt and the crops.

    Life is good with a breeze on your face, the sun to your back, and plowed earth beneath your feet…but watch out for electric fences. When I see one I smile and walk funny.

A new look at family

Before my father died I asked him a question about one of our ancestors and he told me he didn't know the answer and that frankly, there was no one else left to ask. My father had five brothers and two sisters — my father was the youngest. All the siblings were now gone and the joys he use to have reminiscing about his childhood were no longer possible. That door to the past had closed and could never be opened in this world.

Now I sit beside my mother and she points out the names of people in old black and white photographs for me. I see a picture of my grandmother and grandfather but they aren't smiling. They stare into the camera, somber and serious, like the people you see in pictures of the Civil War or the old West. Behind them is one of the fields that made up their farms.

My grandmother died when I was young but I remember her as a quiet woman who always hugged me when we came to her house to visit. I like to imagine that soon after that particular picture was taken she saw us turn into her dirt drive and broke into a smile as my father brought the car to a stop. I tear out of the car, run up to her and give her a big hug around her knees and she makes her usual offer to cook all of us a meal if we're hungry. This is a woman who bore eight children without an epidural. She had some serious energy, and obviously, so did my grandfather.

There's a lot I'd like to know about my ancestors — what did they laughed about, what were they thinking — but they left no record of those things. Photo albums and written memoirs are for the upper middle class. People who've been hoeing tobacco, planting corn, feeding hogs, milking cows and selling meat or running a country store do not sit down at the end of each day and write elaborate thoughts in journals and pose for photographs. They are tired.

Sometimes I think back to my grandmother on my mother's side, Alice, and the time is 1964. She lived in the city and worked for an insurance company and won a trip to the Worlds' Fair in New York City. She took me with her and we traveled on a train! It was the trip of wonders.

I ate in a dining car using real silverware and held my first cloth napkin. Later I sat beside a window and watched small towns and farms go by and never dreamed there was so much land in the world as it passed by my window all day long.

In New York I saw buildings so high that I almost fell over trying to look straight up to the top of them and we paid $3.00 for a hamburger and a drink. My grandmother called that "robbery".

The city never slept and rumbled and beeped with traffic and smelled of cooked peppers and hot bagels. I saw pushcart vendors shouting in strange languages and people walked looking straight ahead, everybody seemed to be going somewhere in a great hurry.

When I came back to Elmhurst School I was the only boy in the fifth grade to have seen New York City. I was worldly, a veteran traveler. A girl asked me if it was true in New York that trains ran beneath the streets and was the Empire State building *a real building* and I said yes, it was true, I had seen it all with my own eyes. I had even eaten a $3 hamburger cooked by robbers.

It was the first time I offered to tell an audience about an original experience and was amazed at how they listened. I liked it.

And that is how God makes writers. You go, you see, and you tell everyone else what happened.

2

Holidays and Other Tribulations

A Dickens of a Christmas Tale

Santa, Thanks for the Email

It's Thanksgiving, Stop Texting and Give Thanks

Thanksgiving Is About Tradition, God Help Us

It's Over, So Button Your Pants

Christmas and the Wonder of It All
Beware the Vacation, Pull Kudzu Instead
An Old Testament View of Vacations
Christmas in July Means Hamburgers and Garland

A Dickens of a Christmas Tale

And so Mr. Scrooge kept Christmas in his heart all year long. In fact he kept so much of it that one day while waddling out of Al's Bakery & Diabetic Supplies holding a double whopper chocolate éclair, he clutched his chest, uttered the words "trans fats," and dropped dead on the sidewalk.

People had come to love Scrooge and when word got out of his demise the whole city turned out to mourn. Even the governor showed up and told people how good a friend Scrooge had been to the poor and disadvantaged and not to forget elections were coming up soon and the state needed a good leader such as the governor himself. A baby appeared from out of nowhere and he kissed it. He also said that he, the governor, never had five mistresses. Then he flew away on an airplane.

Bob Cratchit smiled to himself. He and Scrooge had never seen eye to eye with the handouts Scrooge had been insistent upon giving to the homeless and the orphans. Bob was relieved to not have the old geezer barking everyday about how they ought to be doing more for the poor.

"I worked for what I have," Bob said, and sniffed.

Besides, Bob knew the real money was in politics.

Big Decisions Are Best Made with Hotdogs

Bob took the company out of accounting, went into municipal renovation, and became Subsidized Solutions, Inc. The secret to high quarterly projections was simple — you took a boatload of public money, gutted old dilapidated downtowns, put in new streets, spacious sidewalks, and apartments with balconies featuring hot tubs. You held parades every afternoon with elephants and clowns and colorful floats featuring cartoon and fairy tale personalities. You made sure that at night there was always a fireworks display.

Soon empty shops were filled with niche businesses that might sell curtains and tablecloths made from snowy owl feathers or lady's shoes made from recycled pencil erasers. It caught on and cities throughout the nation began spending millions to renovate. Riding this wave all the way to the bank was the smug Mr. Bob Cratchit, until the EPA took him to US District court for using toxic asphalt traced back to Chernobyl. The streets glowed at night.

"I'm innocent. I didn't do nutin'." said Bob.

The court disagreed and gave him eight years without parole in the federal pen.

Meanwhile, Tiny Tim lost the goody two shoes image. He'd become a lumbering hulk, shaved his head, and had a barbed wire tattoo around his neck. He formed a band, The Broken Legs, changed his name to T&T and wrote songs like "Text U2!" and a ballad called "iPhones and Pills." He played Holiday Inn lounges on the Gulf coast and never had a top selling hit but did appear once on the Jerry Springer show, where just before a soup commercial he physically attacked his third cousin for dating his uncle's niece. No one really got hurt and Springer's rating shot upward.

Tim slowly slid down the slope of dark depression, started sniffing powdered goose down, and ended up in rehab. It was there his life turned around.

While walking to a support meeting, he came upon a hydrangea bush that suddenly burst into flames and began to burn, but the bush wasn't harmed. He heard a voice say, "You're too self-centered. It's not always about you so drop the self-pity, kiddo, and count your blessings. Love you. Now go get a bucket of water, quick."

Tim took his old name back and now he works for a Christian newspaper and writes a column called "Blessings From Above." He also had a bestselling book titled *Hey God, 'Preciate It*. He loves the holidays and spends them with his wife, son and two daughters on their ranch in Colorado. His wife, Carol, says Tim is a wonderful father, cooks a great goose, and on Christmas day you can hear him humming "Silent Night" all the day long.

Santa, Thanks for the Email

Dear Santa,

It's been awhile since I've written to you but now I take pen in hand to thank you for Christmas' past (the chemistry set in '65 was neat — homeowner's insurance did pay for Mom's kitchen) and to ask a favor.

I have three wonderful grandchildren, and I would love for you to make a special appearance this Christmas at their homes. If you could stop by, knock on the door or even come down the chimney and surprise them with your jolly Ho! Ho! Ho! and shake that big belly of yours and bring some special toys, I'd really appreciate it. Oh, and if you could let them see the sleigh and the reindeer — Donner, Blitzen, Cupid, and the rest that would really be a hoot!

Sincerely,
Joe
(Your biggest fan)

Big Decisions Are Best Made with Hotdogs

To: Joehud@hotmail.com
From: Sclaus@northpole.mx.net

Joe,

    Sorry for the delay in answering your letter but our postal mail division was downsized some time ago. We deal mainly with emails or website orders — it's a 30 percent savings over handling postal letters. I was able to get your email address from Facebook.

    Our security people X-rayed your envelope, cleared it then sent it to our Finance Division for their opinion as to the most cost effective way to address this matter. From there it went to our Risk Management division to be reviewed for legal and liability issues. I'm sure you can appreciate our concerns.

    Joe, while I am honored by your request for me to make an appearance for your grandchildren, our Public Relations Division and Accounting has determined it simply is not cost effective for the CEO to make house calls anymore. I do publicity appearances and handle the really big jobs, but these days I'm mostly administration.

    I'm now working with a great bunch of reindeer, but they are currently under contract doing a Discovery Channel documentary (*Reindeer — Animals With Feelings*) and are unavailable at this time. The old bunch is no longer with us. We can't discuss personnel issues but if it's all the same to you I'd forget that bunch of union threatening, hoof stomping, hay eaters (read: JERKS). We have a new contract with a reindeer firm in New Zealand and things run much more smoothly now.

    As far as toys I don't work out of a bag anymore. We now distribute out of Puerto Rico, the Philippines, and India. Elf labor got to be expensive with health care, holiday pay, workers comp, retirement benefits, etc. Besides, the North Pole is on it's way out what with global warming so we're looking at Miami or Brazil for a new headquarters.

We now deliver by automated GPS guided robotic reindeer that deliver the presents right down the chimney within a five-foot radius of a Christmas tree. I can monitor any delivery from my laptop and be on Facebook at the same time. We have gift cards too. LOL!

You mentioned the "big belly." Joe, I'm not the big fat guy I use to be. No, I was weight challenged and decided to face it head-on. I learned that I don't have to be fat and jolly or sustain a stereotype for others. It's time I looked after me for awhile. I admitted to candy abuse, joined a support group, and now I do a lot of cardio workouts and keep a diary of my feelings. I've taken charge of my life and I'm down to 167 pounds. I was motivated to do all this by watching Dr. Oz on TV.

It was good to hear from you. I'll mail you three 8X10 glossies, autographed. Mrs. Claus and I love your column.

Merry Christmas.
Later.
SENT FROM MY WIRELESS BLACKBERRY

It's Thanksgiving, Stop Texting and Give Thanks

A big crowd gathers around a table outside of a store, all waiting to get a book from one of our local authors, Hunter Darden. They look forward to cozying up with her book knowing they shook hands and talked with the author herself. They feel they know her as a friend and not as a pixel TV personality or radio voice. Books and authors are personable; you feel they belong in your home. Ms. Darden was not there to campaign for the whales or warble against bad cholesterol but to simply give pleasure and joy to those that came. She did a great job.

This is similar to the goal for Thanksgiving — to bring the whole family together in one place, have a great time, and hope no one gets chopped through the chest with a meat cleaver.

We are a texting, over-caffeinated, self-absorbed people, but the aroma of turkey, cinnamon, sweet potatoes, and a bucket of butter compels the herd to jostle together at the family table for an amiable occasion. There is always some preachy member that knows the truth about Obama's citizenship or has the real skinny on the Gulf oil spill. A Tea Party wannabe will be there as well as some folks on a diet heavy with basil that will tell you it's changed their life and marriage for the better. They now wear black thongs and feel frisky as rabbits.

The liberals will sit around and tolerate the dim bulbs (Conservatives, those-of-us-who-are-right). The Vegetarian/fish member brings his own platter — a meatless pile that looks like something you don't want to step in. No one asks to try it, which makes him angry — a great excuse to sulk and then be smug about his nose ring, silver tongue stud, and rows of earrings. He looks like a tackle box blew up in his face.

This is the mother of all dinners — that great cook off that is comforting and generous, completely predictable, and creates a spirit of thankfulness for the many blessings we have. These days we seem to be all about complaints and consumption. But this is a day devoted to something else entirely — gratitude and blessings. It's not about us. We all become connected by high carb intake and pounds of cholesterol and our attention finally becomes focused on how blessed we are. Our cars are dependable, the pecan pie never disappoints, and Uncle Carson's gall bladder surgery was a success.

In my day, we had Thanksgiving dinner at my grandparent's home at Hudson's Crossroads — a place where the Bible was the last word, hogs were fed by 7 o'clock every morning, and you could see the dogs under the house through cracks in the floor boards. It was over the Thanksgiving meal I learned my great uncle Lewis Hudson was a physician who became addicted to laudanum (a liquid opium) and that my grandfather John Hudson memorized chapters of the Bible as well as entire newspapers. Good stuff to know.

After the meal we would go outside and run it off. Then late in the evening we would be allowed back into the house, play on the floor, and listen to the adults talk about everyone in church and how the Kennedys were pawns of the Pope. Indeed, these were the last days. Our only hope was Senator Barry Goldwater and why didn't Eisenhower and Patton just kill the Russians when they had the chance? Darn politics, that's why.

Late in the evening our parents would make their way to the door, say goodbye and that would initiate talk in whispered voices about certain family members and my mother would promise to call and check on someone. Then we would drive back home where the dog had to be fed, we took baths, listened to Walter Cronkite, and headed off to bed. I would snuggle beneath heavy quilts and drift off into a dreamless peaceful sleep. Later I would grow up and experience the world with its love, sorrows and joys – sometimes I would stumble and sometimes I would hit home runs. But in those days, I just played and slept.

Be grateful for what you have today because no matter what you think, it is good. Give God thanks and enjoy whatever He has given you. Good luck, God bless, take stock of what you have, and remember to be grateful for every last bit of it.

And keep an eye on that meat cleaver.

Thanksgiving Is About Tradition, God Help Us

A pre-Thanksgiving phone call:

Adult son: But mother —

Mother: No. I want your family to be happy and do what you really want to do. If you don't want to come over for a Thanksgiving meal, I understand — I don't want anyone to feel they have to come on my account —

Adult son: But Mother, we thought just this once Deb would cook the turkey and you —

Mother: I would rather spend Thanksgiving alone than with people who feel forced to sit at my table — the one your father ate at for 58 years.

Adult son: Mother, all I said was—

Mother: I heard you. I would rather sit here alone — on my couch — and eat a frozen turkey dinner than be with people who don't want to be with me.

Adult son: Oh, Mother!

Mother: You know, I should just sell the house — get out of everybody's way, give the money to the church and move into the

Golden Gate retirement home then my children won't have to take time out of their busy schedule...

Adult son (voice catching in his throat): Now please Mother, I didn't mean —

Mother: I'll just go to The Home and make some real friends. You won't be bothered by me anymore. I'll be fine Honey. Really.

Adult son (clutching phone receiver, lying on the floor in a fetal position, sobbing): Momma —Mommy —

Mother: When you come bring some bread. I'm out and I know you love my stuffing. We'll eat at noon.

· · ·

And this is why an entire generation of young women cannot cook a turkey.

Every year new wives and daughters try to lift the burden of holiday cooking from the shoulders of our mothers and grandmothers only to be treated like a potted plant ("Sweetheart, you just stand there in case I need something"). The old matrons, like female elephants in a herd, attempt to maintain control by keeping the secrets of the best water holes to themselves.

Less you consider breaking with tradition you are reminded of your cousin Lindsey. Poor, poor Lindsey. She went rogue in '98 when to her husband's dismay she decided to bake the turkey herself. She studied books on the culinary preparation of turkey, took an on-line turkey baking course, and even joined a Tuesday night support group. She prepared the turkey, set the oven to 350 degrees, and let the bird cook for two and half hours per instructions. No one knows what happened — during its life maybe the bird shot heroin or ate Teflon, who knows — but it came out looking like a mummified Egyptian bird, its baked wings spread as though it had been terrorized at the moment of death. It would have taken the Jaws of Life to cut off a drumstick.

The mother-in-law retired to the living room while Italian music played in the background, and the family took turns bowing and kissing the top of her right hand as Lindsey watched alone from a smoky kitchen. A family member realized Lindsey was watching and quickly closed the door. Now Lindsey lives alone under a restraining order and has a very bad vermouth problem.

But now it's Thanksgiving and you feel a need to contribute so you offer to bring a simple pie, but beware, you may be walking into a minefield. The crust could come out burnt or soggy. Do you own a rolling pin? Have you ever cored an apple? Is your marriage up to this? Suppose the filling tastes like dead hamsters?

For days you ponder the wisdom of baking a pie. You pray about this and then one night while gargling before going to bed, God sends you a vision of a Food Lion supermarket with its wonderful selection of pies — in the frozen section.

You rinse your mouth and smile. You now know what to do. Everything is going to be okay.

Happy Thanksgiving!

It's Over, So Button Your Pants

Christmas is over and everyone is gone. The house is strewn with bits of paper that did not get picked up. A forgotten toy lies beside the dog's dish while in the living room you are slumped on the couch with your legs extended straight out to give your stomach, which now resembles the Louisiana Superdome, more room. You unbutton your pants and appear comatose.

Earlier the crowd arrived and you got to meet family members and after ten minutes you remember why you visit with these people only once a year. You met the young niece's boyfriend Mark, very Gothic in a black leather jacket with a pink streak of hair running across the top of his Mohawk haircut. The nose ring, earring, and lip ring made his face look as though he had fallen in the tackle box. You were delighted to meet him, you said.

There was the one sister that does not get along with a cousin and shows up late just to make a statement. Everyone was seated and eating and now everybody has to get up from the table and hug and kiss her as she comes in with her brood in tow. Her grand entrance made, you go back to your seat, and hope your turkey dressing hasn't gotten cold.

Christmas Dinner is noisy — kids fussing over rarely seen dishes ("No Pop-Tarts sweetie, eat your turkey, yum, its good…now eat…")

Big Decisions Are Best Made with Hotdogs

An uncle loves to talk with his mouth full yet open while he criticizes Obama and directs all of this at you for your viewing pleasure. Someone calls out for the cranberry sauce, the dog starts barking at all the activity, the phone rings, and you jump up to answer it, and it's a relative that couldn't make it but wishes everyone the best. A young father coaxes his daughter to tell what she got for Christmas, and she directs her eyes at you. Now you must stop eating and look her in the face with polite interest while you over hear two brothers-in-law discuss deer hunting, and you hope they don't share tips on how to gut and cut the carcass. Forks and knives scrape against plates; water glasses are picked up and set down making constant bumping sounds against the table cloth and your mother apologizes for her oyster dressing that she claims did not come out right this year. She remembers how your father loved that dressing — her eyes tear up and she excuses herself from the room.

Later, dessert is consumed by future diabetics, and like a defeated army, we throw down our forks and knives, overwhelmed by the sheer volume of food.

Then as soon as dinner is over the Christians leave the table and practice Islam by segregating the rooms by gender. The men all move downstairs to the alters of the couch and chairs while the women stay in the kitchen. Your wife calls downstairs to see if God's chosen need anything. You don't.

But the spirit of Christmas works its magic as you learn the Gothic boyfriend wants to study genetic blindness and how to control it. He is mature, you misjudged and find you like him. The baby sister is considering a teaching position at East Carolina University and a granddaughter loves you, she tells you so, and Christmas is complete. Then the crowd queues up at the front door and takes off, one squadron at a time.

We all got along — no one was stabbed with a carving knife — there was no drama. No one began to cry or shout, "You've never understood how sensitive I am! I've always felt left out in this family!" and fled to the bathroom, slammed the door and fifteen minutes later, after much begging by others, she emerged, sniffling, and was encouraged to write that movie documentary about the suffering of homeless diabetic bipolar musicians. Everyone was sure it would be a wonderful story.

No, none of that happened. You reflect on all of this with a soft belch. Now, if you could just button those pants.

Christmas and the Wonder of It All

This is the week of Christmas, and like a sponge dropped into a bucket of water and left over night, we are all saturated with the holiday spirit. "Felix Navidad" plays in our heads nonstop while we inhale Christmas with every breath. We consume platters of rich foods and the elastic in our underwear refuses to stretch any further.

Our City is decorated with green and red ornaments hanging from lampposts wrapped around with small white lights. Storefronts and windows are decorated with green plastic boughs while soft window lights beckon a person to come in from the cold and lay down some plastic. It's Christ's birthday — with great sales at unbelievable prices.

I was walking downtown one afternoon enjoying the Christmas spirit enhanced by the red, green, and silver street decorations. I became so overwhelmed with the joy of giving that I stopped in a men's store and bought a beautiful shirt and tie. Just for me.

I'm like that sometimes — self-centered. I blame this on my upbringing because society accepts that kind of shuck and jive excuse, and I moved on wondering if a deli down the road had some fresh doughnuts. They did and I bought a dozen and ate about five while I walked to my car. Before arriving home for dinner I ate two more — obviously the result of being raised by emotionally distant parents.

To make up for my parents' mistakes, I took my wife to a nice dinner at one of our fine restaurants. I believe Statesville should advertise our local restaurants more than we do. I have yet to eat at one that is not world-class cuisine. I spent two weeks in New Orleans one time and gained ten pounds and temporarily went on cholesterol medication and a cardiac exercise regime. I know what I'm talking about.

At the restaurant I introduced my wife to the idea of ordering Anything You Want No Matter What It Does To Your Waist We're Hitched For Life, and we both devoured schools of shrimp and herds of beef. We then ordered an apple tart the size of a golf cart tire. When the check came I had visions of me and Bernie Madoff (the Ponzi Meister) sharing a room in the poor house with a straw floor, one rickety table, and two empty rice bowls and cold drafts of winter moving about our feet and rats scurrying about in dark corners.

Earlier in the week, the wife and I went to a drive through nativity scene with real people wearing robes and sandals. I've known the lady playing Mary for years and did not realize that she painted her toenails fire engine red. The cold forced one wise man to wear Nikes but the point was well made. There is more to this life than our selfish motives and gains. Jesus loved us so much He gave up a great life with important angels in a gated community and had pieces of sharp iron pounded through his hands and feet so we could have hope and salvation.

Children stare in wonder at the lights and listen as we adults tell them the magic that can happen on Christmas. We put them to bed with a kiss, and we whisper about reindeer on rooftops then we go downstairs with big watery eyes. We wish they'd never have to grow up and have to deal with a phone company — or pancreatic cancer.

The Nativity story and children nudge me inside, my attitude starts to change and I begin to see Christmas like a child does — a wonder. We selfish types with bad upbringing need this time of year to help keep us in line. Merry Christmas!

Beware the Vacation, Pull Kudzu Instead

Once, I was sitting around in North Carolina holding a telephone and I called a lawyer, a plumber, a teacher, an electrician, a preacher, a truck driver, a pathologist, a mechanic, a politician, a school principal, a brick layer, a landscaper, an architect, a policeman, a baker, a surgeon, a fisherman, a farmer, a technician, a seamstress, a salesman, a photographer, a surveyor, a carpenter, a postman, a banker, an accountant, a veterinarian, a locksmith, and I said, "Hi. Sooo, whatcha doing?"

Turns out 95 percent of them were planning their summer vacations.

Vacations are normally a good thing but you should reconsider — there are hazards. Kudzu is a case in point.

Kudzu, brought to the South to help contain soil erosion, is a good thing, right? But the green serpentine vine now threatens to smother the South no matter how we try to stop it. A little caution and common sense about erosion would have gone a long way. And so it is with vacations.

The woman usually promotes the idea of the vacation as a way of being together to strengthen marital bonds — which at first glance seems a wonderful idea.

However this was the idea in 1981 when my first wife (Note: First. Wife.) suggested we take a two week vacation traveling the beaches of North Carolina, a time which I came to refer to as "The East Coast Death March."

We spared no expense as we ate in the best restaurants and stayed in the finest hotels. I was fascinated by historical sites and nautical museums. I loved to explore shorelines and see the coastal lighthouses and watch ships sail in and out of port. She, on the other hand, honed in on every Belk Department store within ten nautical miles. I informed her we had a Belk's back home and she said, "But this Belk's is different. Here, hold this dress while I try these shoes."

We slowly spent our money, did not enjoy the same sights, and with every mile we soured more and more on each other. She was then and is now a wonderful and caring person with a great sense of humor, but though we were in the same car, we went in different directions.

Things got so shaky I thought that maybe sixty days in a jail would have helped our bonds — that maybe a round of gangrene or cutting sugar cane together under the whip of an evil taskmaster would be an improvement, at least we'd find some common ground. But obviously it didn't work out that way.

My current wife and I once went on a vacation cruise and stopped at an island. I took my milk white body out to the tropical sandy beach and lay down with the intention of applying sunscreen after a short nap. Two hours later I awoke to a world full of pain and deep shades of red and indigo. I had to sleep the rest of the week naked and alone and could not even bear the movement of air across my skin. I learned that when confronted with pain I am an immature, self-centered, resentful person. And I weep a lot.

Men are not wired for vacations, no more than a bear is wired to ride a bicycle in the circus. You can train him of course, but he'd rather be doing what bears do. Men are wired to hunt, not gaze at wildlife. A sitting man is a man planning his next newspaper column or how to climb the corporate ladder as he strategizes each stealthy move through the savannah grass to shoot the alert bull elephant.

Our kids are grown and right now my wife is planning our vacation. We've been married almost twenty years, and it occurs to me that perhaps we should play it safe. I'm thinking we just grill hamburgers, sip ice tea, and maybe pull up some kudzu.

An Old Testament View of Vacations

My dentist, Dr. D. Carroll, a very competent man, looked down and patted me on the shoulder. He had applied a new topical anesthetic to numb my jaw so I would not feel the needle prick of the syringe. Then in an unsure voice he asked his assistant for instructions. Did it take two minutes to numb or could he just stick me now? She said she couldn't remember. There was a moment of dead silence in the room and then both burst out laughing. Dental humor.

I admired that. I am a worrier myself and appreciate a professional approach to anxiety.

I come from a long line of worriers and first cut my teeth on vacations. Nothing fills me with trepidation like planning a week of pleasure and fun. I was raised an Old Testament Baptist and believe that God smites people who enjoy carbohydrates, mingle with pagans, and whoop it up — or as they say, go on vacation.

Therefore I believe that a vacation trip only jeopardizes your future. I'm leery of door handles in public rest areas because you know they have been smeared with germs by the great unwashed masses. You always think of gonorrhea or herpes, which until this moment could not be caught from door handles, but you could be the very first to contract both at the same time and in this way. It will make medical textbooks, YouTube and Twitter. You are packed off barking mad and foaming at the mouth to a nursing home that doubles as a truck stop. You are unfriended on Facebook.

Everyone believes you got it from truck-stop sex, and you are judged guilty without having known the pleasure. Later your brain turns to talcum powder, and you die believing you are Henry VIII. At your funeral public outcry has demanded your casket be shrink-wrapped in plastic and instead of pallbearers, they bring in a forklift and the undertaker wears a toxic waste moon suit. They bury you behind the maintenance shed at the cemetery.

Or perhaps back home your sweet old mother has fallen and broken her hip and is now lying on the kitchen floor feebly using a broom handle to fend off the hungry cat. You see all this in your head just before you sit to take your first bite of Chilean sea bass at a resort in Hilton Head. Heavy sigh.

Or maybe the pipes burst in your upstairs bathroom flooding the house and creating mold. When you return home a week later and open the door you inhale virulent mold spoors. You develop a nagging cough and your fingernails fall off, which turns out to be the result of a fatal Brazilian respiratory disease so rare only three doctors in the country even know the name of it.

You grow sicker and waste away. People hug you tighter than usual, pat your back, and silently mouth over your shoulder to the others in the room "Euuw." Then your wife comes to your bedside one evening to spoon feed you your evening bowl of tepid watery soup. She seems hurried. You notice she is wearing a pearl necklace and a black evening dress with spaghetti straps and a nicely dressed man is looking down at you from over her shoulder, smiling — it's the doctor who diagnosed your disease. You stare at the ceiling and say in a weak raspy voice, "If only I had listened to my Sunday school teacher and never taken that vacation." You become so depressed that later when death comes, you don't know the difference.

So you've already made reservations for your summer vacation? Now you're having second thoughts?

Well, I'm sorry you didn't ask me about it first. Good luck.

Christmas in July Means Hamburgers and Garland

I fought the heat of this July with ice water. I lingered in front of the refrigerator longer than necessary while looking for "something" and dreamed of falling into vats of cold vanilla ice cream. Finally I gave up and turned the air conditioner up to "Nuclear Winter" laid on the couch and thought about December, which then reminded me that we were going to have to take our Christmas decorations down soon. That's right — Christmas hit our house early this year, July 5th to be exact.

My wife Louise, a Cajun from Louisiana is competitive as a junkyard dog over a bone, and has an annual unofficial contest with our neighbor, Carl. Both try to see who can put up Christmas decorations first and Thanksgiving seems to be the starting point. Each year I sit at the table finishing my last helping of Thanksgiving dinner while my wife pulls out Christmas decorations and complains that Carl may skip his dessert and get a jump on her. My wife and I have not eaten Thanksgiving dessert together in ten years.

Kathy, Carl's wife, and I have gotten use to the madness over the years, and we just let the two obsess and run about their respective homes gathering decorations. We figure if it ever gets too wild, we can always employ a mild sedative delivered by tranquilizing darts.

This year we invited Carl and his family to celebrate July 4th with our family and they came with their daughters and their significant others. There were hot dogs, hamburgers, potato salad, blackberry and blueberry pies, and enough laughter to make David Letterman jealous.

Things were going great and then somebody suggested we play Corn Hole.

Corn Hole consists of two platforms, each with a six-inch hole. The platforms are set thirty feet apart. The game is simple. You toss a small bag filled with dried corn at the hole in the opposite platform. It is as simple as eating salted potato chips and just as hard to stop. The game drives competitive people crazy and the more we played the more intense the competition became.

Good-natured dares were made and taken. Jokes were made about each other's ability while players finessed and adjusted their throws. Then out of the blue Carl challenged Louise to a game.

"Loser has to put Christmas decorations up — tomorrow, — and don't be slow about it!" He spit on the ground and squared his shoulders back. My wife went still, the way a panther does just before it strikes.

I said something about this being July and America— but it was all lost in a shriek as my wife accepted his challenge. Her eyes turned a reddish hue. She began to pace back and forth, her jaws snapping open and shut. Carl leered, the edges of his teeth seemed unnaturally pointed. He pawed the earth. The mood changed. Along the street doors slammed shut, children were taken inside and passing cars hurried to get out of the area.

The platforms were set up, corn bag colors were chosen and spectators got behind something, anything that could offer protection. Some made the motion of the cross over their chest and prayed.

The game started. Back and forth the corn bags flew along with insults and snarky jeers. Points were made and then lost as the two played like demons. The humidity caused sweat to pour

Christmas in July Means Hamburgers and Garland

down their faces and arms in small rivulets of water. Each player was determined to win.

Thirty minutes of intense playing saw game advantages won, then lost, and then Carl managed to make a lucky toss and reach the winning number of 21. Louise could not negate the point, and the game ended with Carl declared the winner. He laughed like Boris Karloff. My wife glared.

By noon the next day our house sweltered in July heat but each window was decorated on the outside with green garland and red bows. Our mailbox was wrapped like a big peppermint. The heat would have killed an elf.

I'm lying here on my couch wondering if there is an easy way to get the decorations down without too much work. Then it occurred to me — it's July, maybe they'll just melt.

3

Parents & Family

The Wicked Daddy Giant and the Magic Cow

Mother's Love Is Not Sentimental

Things Getting to You? Put On a Stew

My Mother Is an Iceberg

My Momma Rides Motorcycles and Plays Golf

Confessions of an Empty Nester

My Cousin, My Brother

A Report Card for Adults

Missing Socks — They Want a Life

The Wicked Daddy Giant and The Magic Cow

I was finally cleaning out the closet, you know the one you put off doing in hopes that maybe a tornado or an earthquake will happen and you won't have to do it? This one needed to be cleaned out before environmental remediation became necessary. I bought big industrial size trash bags and began filling them up.

Among other things, I found an old Monopoly game, a paint by numbers kit, a set of cups and saucers, five right shoes (?), a gag gift (back scratcher in a traveling kit) from a Christmas party, a sleeping bag, some old VHS tapes and a squad of lost Confederate soldiers — they shuffled out and headed north towards Virginia. The closet really needed a good cleaning.

Then in the far corner I found the toy. It was a small plastic cow.

I stopped and sat down in the floor and held it in my hand. A door from long ago swung open and memories flew out like birds set free.

The black and white plastic cow was part of a toy barn set we bought for my son many years ago. He was about four years old then— a time when Santa was a big thrill, little piggies could be counted on small toes, and Daddy was more exciting than video games.

The cow never stayed with the barn scene. Instead the cow became part of a small group of toys my son would carry around with him. They became regulars to help him guard the fort from the wicked Daddy giant. My son would build a fort out of blankets and overturned chairs and dare the wicked Daddy giant to come upstairs and do battle. My son would hide in the fort and try to be very quiet between giggles.

I remembered one particular battle of the giant and the cow. I had returned home from a meeting that seemed to last for centuries. I was tired and in no mood for play. My tie was pulled down loose, my white shirt looked like I had worn it for days, and I felt like someone had driven a nail into the top of my head. My son's little head popped around a corner and with a big toothy grin he said, "Daddy, you be the giant and try to get me!" Off he scampered up the stairs. I almost called out that maybe another time would be better, that Daddy was too tired tonight. Instead, I took a deep breath and slowly climbed the stairs to his room.

I yelled, "Fee Fie Foe Fum! I smell a boy named David!" which resulted in hysterical giggles coming from his room. I stomped hard up the stairs, shaking walls, rattling knick-knacks on shelves, and making angry giant noises until I reached the door, turned the knob and entered the room.

"I smell a boy in here that would make good soup!" shouted the wicked Daddy giant. The giant stomped the floor so hard the room shook. Giggles turned to shrieks and the cow was tossed over the fort wall. The cow hit the giant about waist high with barely enough force to be felt then dropped to the floor.

Now everyone knows that wicked Daddy giants cannot fight a magic cow and the giant roared in pain (hysterical laughter from the fort). The giant staggered backward and out the door and warned the little boy that he would get him next time and eat him up! Then the giant went downstairs to find the TV remote.

Now that little boy can drive a car, his legs are hairy and he is filling out applications for college.

The Wicked Daddy Giant and The Magic Cow

I held the cow in my hand, staring at it and I wished that just one more time there was a fort that needed to be taken and a little boy that needed to be eaten in soup. I finished cleaning out the closet but the cow never made it to the trash bag. It has a special place in our house, and that place is known only to the wicked Daddy giant.

Mother's Love Is Not Sentimental

It is amazing that something as wonderful as becoming a mother is not conducive to sentimental memories.

About seventeen years ago I saw a woman become a mother, and believe me, it was not a pretty sight. She was in a room with a doctor and a nurse, her legs were propped up, her damp hair appeared plastered to her forehead from perspiration, her hospital gown was wet around the shoulders, and her lips were pulled back in a sneer of pain.

I asked her, "Does it hurt real bad?"

She gave me a look that would have opened an oyster at twenty paces. She said things about the doctor and me and not one of them was complimentary. The word "epidural" was probably the only word she screamed that is suitable for print.

After nine hours of effort our son finally came and was placed in his mother's arms. She counted his fingers and toes, ran her hands over his bald red head, stroked his cheek, held him close for awhile, and then gave him to the nurse and went to sleep, a pale worn face on a damp pillow. This was not glamorous and over twenty years later has yet to produce any sentimental memories.

Motherhood starts out so nice at first. There are romantic dinners, Sunday drives in the country, some good movies, you talk about things you both have in common, and later the wedding goes okay and you come home from the honeymoon. Then the mothers-to-be begin their slow slide to bonded servant, counselor, cleaning technician, cook, disciplinarian, homework teacher, and supervisor of household transportation.

A woman who might have been a research chemist or a Federal judge swaps her size six or eight dress for a bigger waist and diapers filled with excrement, long hours at night holding a colicky baby, hands that smell like bleach, and all the while losing the potential to be a fashion model on a magazine cover.

Motherhood demands that she give up much of her life so we can have ours. She is poured into life like wet concrete to harden, so we can build our lives on her foundation, she takes the weight. We get to deal with decorating our lives while she supports the floor structure and load bearing walls that our ornaments rest upon. She cleans up what is hurled from the stomach of a sick child while we search for the TV remote.

Mothers love unconditionally even if you use her lipstick to paint the new dinette table, wash the hamster in the toilet with her favorite bath soap, or steal forbidden cookies before dinner. She will kiss the tip of a nose that she has just pulled a green pea out of and can find a Band-Aid at any hour of the day or night.

At a courthouse, you'll see some person being led away by uniformed people. Usually you'll also see an aged woman in the crowd, maybe wringing her hands, looking at the offending person, and she would take them back home in a minute, feed them, clean them up, and try to get them to do better if only they'd listen to her. She would do this over and over. She's a mother.

Mothers do not become pretty as life goes on — instead they become beautiful and I'm glad. Pretty comes and goes, it's fleeting and dependent upon accessories, hair dyes, and membership at a good gym. But true beauty has its own features like ridge lines on majestic high mountains that have withstood everything life can throw at them yet only become more grand and beautiful from the effort.

My mother is now seventy-nine and chugs up steep gradients on her own steam. Her lines have become graceful and her beauty is that of a solid and sure character. She is not just a grand mountain to look at; my mother is a long chain of beautiful mountains that I'll never see all of but am surprised to discover new insights of forgiveness and witness new heights of love that cannot be imagined.

Which is all well and good, however, I'm still not going to tell her about stealing the cookies.

Things Getting to You? Put On a Stew

March is a mischievous month and a time of climatic mood swings — a sharp reminder that winter is not yet over. And I'm glad.

In a society as complicated as ours, I embrace the simplification winter brings us. Winter shows you that the essentials of life are heat, food, shelter, and a good decongestant. Everything else is fluff.

Weather bound inside our homes with nothing much to do, we listen to the media tell us that homelessness is up, terrorists are at the back door, big corporations have no heart, the jobless rate will only increase, private businesses will fail, and there is no hope for next year. Everyone gets stressed out, their blood pressure rises — they fall down the mineshaft of depression.

Not me, I cook.

Winter stews are a favorite of mine because they require hands-on attention. You can't handle an AK-47 automatic and blow away twenty people at the mall if you're home peeling potatoes — simple logistics. So you stay home and pull out the big pot that is kept out in the garage on top of the outdoor refrigerator and head back into the kitchen.

There is nothing more peaceful than preparing the ingredients for a stew. You've taken your mind off of yourself and spend time with things gentle and quiet like celery, onions, and some quality

Russets. You rummage in the pantry and find two cans of tomatoes, thaw out a chuck roast, and you're ready to go. The neat part is you get to handle a twelve-inch meat cleaver. People coming through the kitchen take care not to rattle you as you bring the cleaver down hard and whack off a six-inch chunk of raw red meat.

Family members pass through the kitchen, maintain distance, and say things like, "Whoa! (hands go up in the air) Sorry to bother you, Dad. On second thought — I'll just work my way through college on my own. Gotta run." And "Honey! Sorry about using all the hot water. I'm headed to my hair appointment — love your shirt." She never takes her eyes off you as she backs out the door. They've been watching you all week and know that right now, you're very fragile.

Cutting up the smaller ingredients brings calm. You change to a chef's knife and your hands work together as you chop celery, dice garlic, and remember that the onions have to be sliced a certain way. You have to pay attention, focus — you want to get the seasonings just right.

You assemble a wonderful assortment of items that will soon blend under heat and send hearty aromas into all parts of the house. You stand quietly before the stove and stir the pot. You realize you have a home, you have food, and, you have shelter. You realize you have a lot to be thankful for, Jack.

The fact of the matter is we are all in deep water, and we know it. Our tax refunds come courtesy of the Chinese, people who hate us control our gasoline, politicians run our lives from dawn until dusk, and our current Chief Executive, a politician, wants to manage private corporations. God help us — and so far He has.

We can't do anything about the weather or make greedy men honest or figure out that mess in the Middle East. The Bible tells us to leave all that up to God — He doesn't vote or negotiate. He has been known to burn things.

But you can prepare a good stew for those you love — gather your family around the table and as the winds outside howl, give thanks. That, you can do.

My Mother Is an Iceberg

One Saturday morning I went out the front door to pick up the morning newspaper and noticed someone had left us a bag of apples. Now you can't let a bag of apples go to waste so I figured I'd do a little cooking. I checked my favorite cookbook, an old Betty Crocker first edition with the spine coming apart, and settled on deep-dish apple pie.

This is like anything else someone brings you, such as a box of oranges at Christmas. You stare at it for a while and think of decent ways to get rid of it. Last December, I put half a box of oranges in the refrigerator and the other half I scattered out back. Dozens of gentle birds descended into my yard — and then began to fight. It looked like a reenactment of Gettysburg.

I'm in the kitchen wearing my grilling apron that has a picture on it of Mickey Mouse holding a spatula. It was a gift to me from my sons bought long ago on a Disney vacation. I finished making my pie crust (yep, I make my own), filled the pan, and placed the pie in the oven.

Out of three siblings I was the only one that hatched with a desire to cook. As a boy I loved to hunt and would bring home rabbits and squirrels to be gutted and cleaned for cooking. Mother taught me how to fry meat and later to make biscuits and stews. She nourished my love for cooking.

Suddenly, I missed my mother like crazy.

I grabbed the phone and called and got her usual "Hi, how are you?" and "What a pleasant surprise!" and "Doctors don't know everything. Keep putting baking soda on it." I listened to her tell me about the weather (it's not normal) and the list of all she was cooking for the church's Homecoming meal. I laughed and quoted scripture about gluttony and lascivious living, and told her I could picture her dancing around a golden calf and waving a stick of butter in the air. She sighed and said that she'd always regretted not spanking me more.

Then without skipping a beat she went on about people who had recently died. She named a lady I was not familiar with. Who?

"Oh, she was sweet. She was an administrator for the city. When I graduated high school she offered me the City Clerk position."

"But Momma, you never went to college. How did you know people in city government? You lived on a farm."

Well, it seems my little mother had been a "brain" in high school and was offered financial assistance to obtain a college degree. Trouble was, she fell in love with my father, it was the late 1940s, and he wanted her to stay home.

Why?

Because he did. That's why.

She told me she had also always wanted to study law. Even now at seventy-seven years of age she thinks about that decision. For over an hour she told me about the lost dream of having a professional career.

I never knew that about her.

I smiled and imagined — Momma Esq., of Baptist, Bible & Hudson. She would have made judges sit up straight and felons eat soap.

It occurred to me that people are like icebergs. We see only a small part and we would swear we've seen all there is yet there is so much more unseen below the surface. What a delightful surprise to discover a new dimension of someone you love. Those are the things that make life the wonder God intended it should be.

I thought about my mother all day long and imagined her as an accountant, a CEO and then as a lawyer. I was tempted to take her a pie — as a retainer fee.

My Momma Rides Motorcycles and Plays Golf

Doris, my mother, is going to play golf.

Now that statement in itself probably does not cause you alarm but remember a small puff of wind off the coast of Africa can become a hurricane and make 100,000 people evacuate their homes in New Orleans. To say my mother is going to take up golf is akin to that small puff of wind, the storm could be a big one.

Momma is barely four feet ten inches tall, has osteoporosis, taught Sunday school for over forty years, and drives herself anywhere whenever she chooses. I call her about three or four times a week and just hope I catch her at home.

I should not have been surprised then when she informed me this week that at the age of seventy-seven she intends to take up golf. She said this like you'd say you were going to run to the store for some milk. My mother did not get to where she is today by just baking sugar cookies.

She reads the Bible for hours, could get her deer every season if the mood struck, drives for hours just to shop, cleans her house from top to bottom weekly, drives her golf cart around the farm, cooks her own meals, can tell you where the public school system went belly up, and then ask you "Would you like a BLT sandwich for lunch, Honey?" My mother has life by the horns.

Mother was the guest speaker at the Golden Scriptures Bible group one Wednesday morning when she mentioned she'd like to lose about ten pounds, Lord willing, and that she was no good at dieting — it takes too long. A slim, elderly lady walked up to her after the meeting and suggested she take up golf and the lady herself would teach her if mother were so inclined. My mother agreed. I've no doubt God moaned and the number of angels assigned to my mother doubled. God and I have seen her work.

When I was twelve years old I walked into the kitchen one day while this staunch Baptist lady was washing dishes. I announced to her that no one really knew if God existed and just because a preacher said the Bible was true did not make it so. Maybe Hitler had been right, perhaps his ideas had needed time to gain traction and maybe he had been a smart misunderstood man.

She put the dishes down and told me to get in the car. We drove all the way across town to the Shepherd Memorial Library. She checked out Hitler's *Mein Kempf*, we drove back home and she handed me a dictionary and her Bible.

She said, "Read this so you'll be informed, not ignorant. Then tell me what you think."

To this day I have a Bible at my office, several in the house, and I'm glad Hitler's dead.

I bought a motorcycle when I was sixteen and brought it home. My father said it was a waste of money, and my sister said I'd be dead in a week— could she have my room? My mother stood there in a white shirt, faded blue jeans and white sneakers. She had never even been close to a motorcycle, but she seated herself on the back and said, "Have me back in time to cook supper." We rode all over Pitt County laughing the whole time.

She can boil and freeze sweet corn all day and still make the 7 p.m. prayer service at church.

With lots of grit this woman has raised three kids, advised preachers and county commissioners, and taught more Baptists in Sunday school than the Devil has lobbyists. And now she is eyeing the PGA.

She asked me how many strikes you get at a golf ball.

"It's not strikes Momma," I said. "It's strokes and you normally get only one at the ball when you tee off."

"Well," she said and looked up at me, hands on her hips, "that's dumb. I would have to take more. Problem?"

I felt a small puff of wind, and I honestly believe that I heard the frantic beating of angel's wings.

Confessions of an Empty Nester

A beautiful morning, the first day of school, and a crowd of nervous talkative children huddle in clusters waiting to board a yellow school bus. Their mothers hug them and give last minute instructions and assurances of love. These kids from decent homes are being sent off to the world of state managed education and God-only-knows what. The mothers watch their kittens board the bus, some mothers dab tissues at their eyes. A thousand thoughts go through a parent's mind. Has the driver had a background check? Does he have a license? You suppose he's a serial killer? Sober? What about falling asteroids? Are the axles on tight? Should we kick the tires? Anybody checked the lug nuts?

I sympathize. I am an Empty Nester.

Recently I abandoned my son on the doorstep of a university and prayed the same Parent's Prayer I have prayed since the day he was born, "Lord have mercy. Please God, have mercy." You suddenly realize the little bundle of gas, poopy diapers, acne, trumpet lessons, church camps, and soccer tournaments has grown up. Now he has legal rights, long hairy legs, and can tolerate yeast-based liquids.

We helped him unload the things we had bought for him to start his new life — blankets, sheets, pillows, detergent, a lamp, clothes, toiletries, and most of all, a credit card from the First Bank of Dad. We finished settling him in and then he said goodbye. At that very instant I realized that he had flown the nest. The days of saying "No" were over. The times of wondering where he was, were over. Now he would have to know where he was. Now, he would have to say "No" of his own accord. Lord have mercy. Please God, have mercy.

As we walked back to our car my wife tried to hold it together. Her bottom lip quivered as she got into the car.

I told a friend about this some days later.

"It was a long hour and a half drive," I said, " in a small car with close seats sitting beside a grown adult who was crying into tissues, wracked by sobs, weeping — the constant sniffling and swollen red eyes."

"Goodness!" said my friend. "But I'm sure you were a source of strength for your wife."

"My wife?" I replied. "I was talking about me! My wife was great — she held my hand the whole time. I was a train wreck."

Relinquishing parenthood is tough. You've gripped it so long and so hard it takes effort to release the hold you've had on the rudder of responsibility — guiding a life through choppy waters and now you've reached the harbor. You tie the boat to the dock and walk away.

But there is some consolation. I find the cash in my billfold stays there until I spend it, and our bathroom actually has a nice tile floor – I thought it was made of blue jeans, T-shirts, and damp towels. I found my old razor, missing since '08, and when we buy food and put it in our kitchen, it's there until we eat it — ourselves.

The truth is I can't wait for him to come home to visit and park his car in our driveway. We'll fawn over him — cook whatever he wants and dote on him hand and foot. And when everyone has gone to bed that night, ol' Dad in a thin bathrobe and slippers, will sneak out to his son's car and while no one is looking, see to the tires and quietly check the lug nuts.

My Cousin, My Brother

My cousin Randy died in his bed at his farm in eastern North Carolina while I was in Virginia making plans to go to Charleston. I cleared my calendar and drove the four hours in time for the funeral service. When I left to return home, I crossed the Tar River and remembered the times he and I fished for Bluegills and hunted squirrels in the nearby woods. We grew up together in the woods, and on the creek banks, and on the farms, and in our church, and all around the community.

About a year ago he noticed coffee cups and china plates were getting heavy which is strange for a red-haired guy that could land a ten pound bass, sell insurance, operate a farm and lift grandchildren for a kiss on the cheek. He went to the doctor and was diagnosed with amyotrophic lateral sclerosis — Lou Gehrig's disease. A loving intelligent mind became trapped in a body that gradually ceased to move, talk or swallow. His family administered to his needs, they prayed and hovered about like angels until the real ones came.

Randy and I did everything together. We hunted rabbits and always sat side by side in Sunday School. We played checkers and guitars and shot hoops together. We practiced blowing smoke rings behind the barn, and we shared banana sandwiches.

He and I almost died together once when we were twelve years old. We had been told to be careful when driving tractors and never use the highway gear in a field as the tractor would go too fast and possibly overturn — so naturally when our fathers weren't around, we used the highway gear and drove as fast as we could.

We were barreling across a field, Randy was hanging on the back and we were laughing, barely able to keep the bouncing tractor under control. Suddenly ahead was a deep empty canal used to drain the fields during wet weather. I tried to throttle back but the jostling of the tractor caused my hand to miss the throttle. We were poised to plunge into the canal and possibly be crushed beneath the tractor.

I kicked the left brake pedal hard trying to make the tractor pivot and change course. Randy reached around to help turn the steering wheel but too late, we saw one of the front wheels of the tractor swing out into mid-air. The canal bank beneath us began to cave in.

Miraculously the left back wheel anchored causing the tractor to turn on a dime and swing away from the canal, almost flinging us off in the process. Somewhere in the distance I heard girls screaming — then realized it was us.

I throttled back, hit both brakes and shut off the engine.

We were safe.

We stared at each other, barely breathing, our mouths hanging open. Then one of us giggled, then one snorted, and a ripple of giggles turned to waves of hysterical laughter and we laughed and laughed and pointed at each other and laughed even harder.

Not everyone is lucky enough to have a cousin who becomes a brother — I was blessed.

When your brother dies, your childhood begins to fade as there is one less person to remember it with and you feel disinherited, abandoned, a lone wanderer. It's like losing the hard drive in your computer and there is no back up — none.

He was buried in the family cemetery that was not far from the field where we'd driven the tractor long ago. While everyone prayed I stared across to that field, and though I couldn't see him — my eyes were too watery — I'm sure I heard him laughing.

A Report Card for Adults

This morning I was in mid-sip of fresh brewed Columbian coffee when my son walked into my office and handed me his report card for my signature. Like any all-powerful parent I stared at him and with great purpose put down my cup and motioned for him to give me the document. I read it, noticed the A's and one B. I raised an eyebrow and stated that the B needs to become an A. Then like an old army supply sergeant I hefted a pen in my hand and with a show of authority and flourish signed my name and handed the report back to him. He left the room and as I watched him go down the hall I had two thoughts:
1. How proud I was of him.
2. How glad I am that grown-ups do not receive report cards.
    I imagined what horror a report card on a self-centered crusty adult like me would look like:
    Appearance: Joe's blood pressure is up and his stomach is hanging down. He has gained twelve pounds this semester. Continues to ignore diet and exercise. Needs improvement.
    Conduct: Joe elbows people away from the lunch table if Buffalo wings, potato chips or chocolate cake is being served. Joe has been known to trample over small children if ice cream is present. Joe is inconsiderate and blames others for faults regarding his decisions

and has been caught smoking an occasional cigar in the back yard. Blames lack of sleep for his laziness yet insists on rising each morning at 4 o'clock to write folksy columns and essays that he thinks are witty and entertaining. He is harmless but tends to be self-indulgent and will not share the TV remote. Needs improvement.

English: Likes it but tends to ignore grammar. His editor has complained. Example: "Ain't got time." Not a proper sentence — uses slang. Needs improvement.

Foreign Language: Has yet to master English.

Math: Clearly shows no interest. See un-reconciled bank statements.

Art Appreciation: A very disappointing semester. Joe does not understand that the Sunday color comic strips are not American interpretations of Monet paintings.

Physics: Fails to understand limits of such laws and as a result is on a first name basis with local EMS staff. Demands the ambulance driver operate "all them lights" when transporting him to medical care facilities.

Political Science: Claims nausea at the mere mention of the subject and is sent to detention for use of improper language and gestures.

Religion: Joe made the preacher cry.

Phys. Ed.: Claims it goes against his religion. See above comment.

General Observations: Joe is dull witted compared to his peers and shows little promise of being an asset to the community. He is highly opinionated and defensive. He daydreams and composes silly stories during free time. Suffers from a need to be accepted, is afraid of rejection, and is afraid to accept or reject the reality of either issue. We recommend stronger parental guidance, spiritual tutoring, shock treatment, therapy, soy milk, non-caffeinated drinks, no TV for a month, and the use of behavioral drugs in large quantities.

I would then take this report card and present it to my spouse who would, no doubt, glare at me. I would promise to do better and commit to putting the toilet seat down after use (being considerate of others). Then as I turned away — I would grin.

A Report Card for Adults

Let the kids suffer report cards. As it is now, I am going to sit on my deck with a bag of Lay's potato chips and — knowing that no report card is forthcoming — be me.

Missing Socks — They Want a Life

There are a lot of unsettling moments in life. Like the time you first realized your parents had a life before you, and what they had to do in order to make you and so the next time you sit at the table together to eat, there is awkwardness. Then there was the first time you saw the movie *Love Story* and Ali McGraw died. You sat there sobbing uncontrollably with tears streaming down your face and hugged anyone within ten feet of you, and then stood outside the theater vowing to never take anyone for granted again and then you called your dear old mother as soon as you got home and told her, yes, the whole family will be there for Christmas this year. But nothing quite unsettles you like standing in front of the laundry basket in your underwear ten minutes before you have to leave for work and realize you are missing a sock.

You stand there holding one lonely sad sock. You both feel abandoned — incomplete. Did you say something wrong? Did a sock take offense? You might have mentioned you wished the length was ankle high when they were actually above-calf but you were just kidding — you meant nothing by it. No matter, a sock has gone AWOL, vamoosed — missing.

There should be a committee, perhaps the American Committee for the study of Escaping Socks (ACES) to address this issue. This type of behavior could be called "Provoked Sock Movement" or PSM. No doubt university stockingologists would say there are reasons for PSM and they go deep.

We forget that socks are forced into a life of drudgery. They are stretched and pulled over yellow gnarly toenails or feet ripe with athlete's foot. Socks are forced over large bunions and toe jam that smells like bad mayonnaise. Sometimes a sock is crammed into shoes too small and forced to absorb sweat all day. Do we ever say "Thank you, Sock"? No, we assume they will be there when we need them.

Being taken for granted can affect a relationship — just ask your spouse. Therefore we should not be surprised when one lone sock has had enough and calls it quits.

Remember times at night when you think you hear a bump or soft scampering but figured it is nothing so you turn over and go back to sleep? Actually that was a sock making an escape.

The next morning you walk by a clothes drawer that is partially open. You could have sworn you closed that very same drawer yesterday. If you look closely you'll notice the drawer is open just enough for — yes! — a sock to squeeze through. The hair rises on the back of your neck and you wonder just how close it crawled by you last night on its way out. Be sure to check your wallet for missing bills.

Where do socks go?

Some socks leave to find religion or go into therapy or join cults. Many become damaged or unravel in the attempt to escape and end up behind a washing machine or dryer. They were drawn there out of familiarity and could not make the climb up to the outside dryer vent. Months later you move the appliance for cleaning and the socks are found lying there flat, dust coated, and shriveled.

Escaped socks sometimes die by roads and highways. Occasionally you will see one on the side of the road or lying on a traffic island by an interstate highway. Some look vaguely familiar — the "missing" brown Argyle? But the rains have pounded it flat, and now its threads are left to be bleached by the sun. It's not a pretty sight.

Missing Socks — They Want a Life

Socks that leave or are "missing" are trying to be an individual and have a full life and when you think about it, that's a lot like us. So as you start your day consider those that make your steps easier — be they human or sock. Say "Thank you," tread lightly, and be nice.

4

Traveling

Daddy Hugs Away the Nightmares

When In a Marriage, Plans Change

The Young Never Change, Thank Goodness

The World Needs More Southern Gentlemen

I'm Motorcycling Out of Father's Day

Be Pleasant, Be Sweet, Be Southern!

Daddy Hugs Away the Nightmares

There is an unwritten rule among boys that crying is something you avoid at all costs. We somehow assume we are tough, manly, and in control if we do not show that we have tear ducts.

You grow up as boy somehow knowing this and so when the time comes it's a big deal. A kid can lose or gain his standing with his group. It's a rite of passage and you understand that no matter what happens, you must not cry. My first test, as all first tests of growing up do, came suddenly and unexpectedly. Greg, a buddy of mine, and I were sitting around the back yard one day trading baseball cards and making dares. He dared me to let him give me an Indian burn. He grabbed my forearm and with both hands he twisted the skin in opposite directions. Hard. It burned and hurt like crazy and I clinched my jaws. But hey, I passed, no tears.

A bigger test came one day when five of us were hanging out during third grade recess period. Someone said that a tough guy could take a hit in the stomach and not cry or flinch. So everybody lined up and took a hit to the stomach. When my turn came a kid named Radford gave me a moment to "tighten up" and then he hit me in the gut but his aim was off and instead of my stomach he hit me in the middle part of my rib cage close to my heart. My ribs felt like they had been hit with a jackhammer and my heart, for a moment, ached and felt like it was in a tight vise. I *saw* white pain! I wanted to bend down and cry but instead I stood there, stoic, screaming and hurting on the inside but I shed no tears. I remember my heart aching, feeling bruised all day.

And life marched on.

Recently I was taking a break from a motorcycle ride at a small park a few miles off the Blue Ridge Parkway. I came upon a birthday party in progress and sat at a picnic table to the side and watched.

A group of boys that appeared to be about ten years old were playing softball. Periodically one of the boys would break from the game and run over to an old man who was standing within hearing distance of me. The kid wanted to know when he could open his presents. The old man, apparently his grandfather, kept telling him to be patient. The little guy did this, over and over, and each time the old man said, "Wait, just a bit longer." The boy ran back to the game and the old man would always look up the highway, expecting.

About thirty minutes later a green Ford Explorer came down the road, its big tires rumbling over gravel and throwing up a cloud of dust behind it as it slowed and pulled into the parking lot. The passenger door opened and out stepped a man in military fatigues and boots. He looked like he had been wearing them for a while.

His uniform was wrinkled and you could see sweat patches under his arm. There were small holes and tears in the uniform and small areas of yellow dirt on his shirt and pants. His boots were dusty and worn.

The game stopped — everything stopped. The birthday boy was at bat and stared at the soldier. Suddenly the air seemed charged. Women who were laying out food stopped, covered their mouths with their hands, mothers tending small children in carriages or sandboxes stood up straight and looked toward the soldier. Men who had been lying on their sides under shade trees smoking cigarettes suddenly stubbed them out in the dirt and stood up.

I looked back at the boy.

The bat that had been on the kid's shoulder slowly slid to the ground. I realized the man with the Explorer was the boy's father, and I waited to see the expected smile.

Instead the boy stood rock still. I heard the bat hit the ground. The corners of his mouth turned down, his forehead wrinkled, and then tears suddenly gushed out of his eyes. His little mouth opened but nothing came out. I've never witnessed a scream so silent. His little arms and hands went up and down as though he didn't know what to do with them.

I can still see his arms and hands.

Adults forget that kids have worries, concerns, and fears yet they have no wife, no husband to tell them to. A kid cannot articulate the fear that his father might be shot and never come back home. Kids have to live quietly with their nightmares and scream and cry into their pillows. They see and hear the news of the war, and we expect them to be normal, behave — play ball! The boy's moving arms and hands were dropping loads of unbelievable burdens, bad dreams, and silent fears.

I then realized the kid's head was shaved, just like his father's. A choking sound came out of the boy's mouth and he bolted, he ran straight to his daddy, little thin arms and hands moving up and down — little thin arms and hands dropping nightmares and fears and cries and loneliness and fright.

The big soldier dropped to his knees and grabbed his son. The man's big arms wrapped around the child as though to shut out the rest of the world and never let go. He kissed his son's head, ears, cheeks and neck. The boy had found his voice and was sobbing "Daddy! Daddy! Daddy! Oh, Daddy!" The boy buried his face in his father's neck and the big man's shoulders began to shake. I heard a deep loud sob, almost a wail come out of the father that went out and up into the air and beyond the mountaintops.

I suddenly felt the place where Radford had hit me many years ago, so close to my heart, and was surprised to find that after all these years, the tears had finally caught up with me.

When In a Marriage, Plans Change

Marriage veterans will agree that to help a marriage sometimes you have to get away from all the blessings that come with it. Those would be the seventeen-year-old son (his two brothers are out of the nest), a boxer dog, laundry, bill paying, grocery shopping, oil changes in the cars, picking up clothes, doctor appointments, lost socks, etc.

My wife and I were weary of our blessings.

Therefore we made plans to get away for some "us" time. You know, that time you wonder, "when was the last time" kind of time?

We decided to go to our cabin in the mountains for a weekend. Our son is old enough to call in pizza and feed the dog. I gave him some twenties — he wouldn't starve and the dog would have a fifty-fifty chance.

The fly in the ointment was the fact that we were both coming down with colds. My wife catches those chest coughs that threaten to hurl her lungs out onto the floor and me, I'm a sinus guy — I stop up tighter than a clogged stadium toilet. We both wished we felt better and I forgot to bring a heavy coat and she forgot to bring a new recipe to try.

While we rode we talked about the kids, furniture we'd like to buy, and what we'd do if we won the lottery. She said she'd set up a trust for the boys, pay off all the bills, and buy us a nice house on a farm.

I said I'd buy a new motorcycle, and drive up to Alaska just me all by myself and see the bears.

Dead silence.

My bad.

M'Lady allowed that if I needed so much alone time, without her, I could shag my motorcycle self to Alaska right now. The bears would probably love to see me too — about lunchtime. And, she continued, did I realize how self-centered I was and that I was always like that about things? I was informed that the world does not revolve around me. I tried to appear like I knew that.

We drove in silence — a lot of silence. It was the silence that only married people can produce when a mood sours. I studied the brake lights of a truck ahead of me, and she turned on the radio and looked out the window at the darkness. Her cough was growing worse; my throat was raw.

After 31.7 miles I said that what I'd really like to do would be to buy a sidecar for the motorcycle and she could ride with me for eternity and that I always thought Elizabeth Dole should be president. Why did that sound like an apology?

She chuckled and turned the radio off. My nose was running — I needed some tissue and she found some in her purse. We started talking again, this time about remodeling the kitchen.

The road to the cabin was narrow so I drove very slowly as quarter size snowflakes floated down from the night sky. She coughed, I sneezed — we were both feverish and decided that our original plans for recreation, sans clothes, would be put on hold. We felt awful and coughed like patients in a Tuberculosis ward.

Then, around a curve, three beautiful deer emerged out of the snow and crossed the road in our headlights. They stopped and so did I. You could see their soft brown eyes, snow had already settled on their backs. They began moving again with such gentle grace they seemed to be mere wisps of brown. We "oohed" and "aahed" like little kids. When the deer had melted into the woods, I released the brake and we slowly started moving again.

We finally arrived, I pulled into the driveway and we got out of the car. We held hands and helped each other walk in the snow. She said there was some cold medicine in the downstairs bathroom and that she'd sleep upstairs — I could sleep downstairs — that way we wouldn't keep each other up being sick. I told her I would cook breakfast tomorrow, and we could watch it snow. She coughed and said she would like that.

We walked towards the house. I squeezed her hand three times real fast and she squeezed mine back.

The Young Never Change, Thank Goodness

A sunny day in the high seventies, a blue sky dotted with cotton ball clouds, and a light southern breeze, and of course I should be discussing national failing health care, the proposed streetscape for downtown Statesville, or the plight of the Polar Bear.

Instead, I'm walking on the campus of the University of North Carolina in Charlotte and enter the student union for a cup of coffee. I'm here regarding some consultation work and hope to connect with my son who is suppose to be making me giddy with pride over his academic accomplishments. I've not heard from or seen him since I paid his tuition many weeks ago. He would be annoyed if he knew I was on campus right now, a thought that makes me smile.

I sit beside a table of students who despite the mounting national debt and lousy job market seem as ebullient as ever. They are discussing what to do for fall break. I overhear a young man in a gym tank top with his flat stomach and defined biceps tell a young lady that he is planning to go hiking in Oregon. She asks him, "How are you getting there?" and Mr. Flat Belly says, " I dunno, maybe hitchhike or catch a ride with somebody."

Yes! Yes! Yes! The young never change. That is exactly how we use to think and talk in the olden days before college graduates were saddled with mortgage size debts. In my college days we talked about hitching rides, did not know what "planning" meant, and discussed escaping from wherever we were, willing to cast our fate to the wind. We believed we could do anything and that having an exciting life and going to exotic places would happen…oh… probably by the afternoon.

It suddenly occurred to me that I have not seen a college hitchhiker in ages — what with serial killers roaming the interstates and homeless people getting the good spots at exit ramps while holding cardboard signs. (Will work for food. Please Help. No windows or yards. God Bless.)

I want to jump up and shout to those kids at the table, "Go right now kid before you get high blood pressure and a mortgage and a list of regrets about chances never taken!" But I don't. I am afraid he might bolt and miss his mid-term exams.

On the other side of my table sit three girls. They are discussing a boy and whether one of the girls should text him or maybe 'go out' with him. These young people flash messages like frantic fireflies — ready to swarm at will. They have their own signals and language. I wondered how *Love Story* would have played out if Ryan O'Neal and Ali McGraw had cell phones with texting, and Ali made the first call like girls do these days.

"WSUP?"
"MISS U"
"DOC SEZ I SIK :-("
"U R 2 AWSUM 2 B SIK :-)"
"LY 4EVER"
"L8R"

I think the story would have moved faster, there would have been less brooding over the outcome, and people would not have cried so much. Abbreviated reality — no fluff — works for me.

I sip coffee and think of fluffy gaseous politicians chanting spells to raise the economy from the dead. This requires spin wizards and lies, all of which my generation seems to have in abundance.

The Young Never Change, Thank Goodness

The students gather their books move away and leave me staring into my coffee.

I smile and feel hopeful about the future — it hangs with these optimistic energetic young people. They have their own language, they own tomorrow and I bet that kid gets to Oregon.

L8RG8R (Later, gator)

The World Needs More Southern Gentlemen

Some people have an uncontrollable need to be first. Manners usually get trampled in the process as demonstrated by a stocky, black-haired lady in the Milwaukee airport who cut in front of me at the boarding gate. She was a practiced Line Cutter, real smooth as she planted her left foot in front of my right foot, lunged forward and without any apology whatsoever, cut me off. I had to stop suddenly which caused the gentleman behind me to accidently nuzzle the back of my neck. Awkward.

To my knowledge, boarding an airplane was not a contest. No one was giving out prizes.

Like a salmon leaping upstream she maneuvered and jostled around people who got in her way all to sit on an airplane for three hours in a very small seat — and from the size of her rear dorsal fin it was going to be a very tight squeeze.

There was a time when I would have wanted to punch her in the nose, pull her hair out, and give her a lecture on manners, but not now. Those days are long gone. You can step on my blue suede shoes, Big Momma, just don't hack into my computer, steal my iPad, or kick my dog.

Big Decisions Are Best Made with Hotdogs

I was raised in the South by Buddy and Doris Hudson, two people who believed in the Bible, fried food, and good manners. Being a Democrat was optional but highly encouraged.

Mother created a desire for politeness by using a Belk-Tyler yardstick for spankings. The woman was like a magician — the stick would suddenly appear out of thin air whenever a "polite manner" was temporarily forgotten. We used "thank you," "yes ma'am," and "no ma'am" like shields.

In the South bad manners are considered boorish. We are taught to hold the door open for those behind us. We give the nod to a stranger if it's a tie for who arrived first at the counter in the auto parts store.

Sometimes we may get very enthusiastic about manners. You open the door and let someone else be the first to step out on the ice-covered sidewalk. When, flat on their back they look up surprised, you assist them to their feet while repeating the Southern mantra, "Bless your heart." Again, it's about being polite.

The world needs more Southern Gentlemen. Without us who will help get your car off the cinder blocks, be governor of Mississippi, or sustain the demand for chrome?

Who's going to take care of old dogs with rheumy eyes, repair long orange drop cords with black electrical tape, and draw the line at canned biscuits? I'm just asking.

Southern men pay taxes, fly airplanes, build large buildings, fight in wars, change tires, write songs, tithe at church, honor our parents, send email, give blood, author books, and we'll even help dig post holes. Southern gentlemen are not ashamed of God or to teach their children manners, and we don't apologize for it.

But it's painful to see others inch ahead of you in a promotion, receive a windfall inheritance, or always get their deer the first day of every season. And yet First Place is not always the best seat in the house. Our heavenly Father says the race is not always to the swift nor the battle to the strong.

First Place can be elusive, even fickle, and it's not always satisfactory when you get there so let the lady jump ahead. You be polite, Sugar Cakes, and allow grace, faith, hope and love to find you the perfect seat. You'll enjoy it a lot more.

I'm Motorcycling Out of Father's Day

Father's Day is here and therefore I am gone. I have taken the weekend off, and I'm not even going to cut the yard. I feel my roots calling me back to the sea, the beautiful sea, and all I need is a ship with good sails, a barrel of hard tack biscuits, and the bright northern star to steer by.

But I'm in Statesville, NC., three hours from the coast.

So I'll climb on my black BMW motorcycle and head due west for the Smoky Mountains and pick up some county road and ride for a couple hundred miles. I'll throttle up that 1100cc engine and let it run free like a wild stallion until I finally come to some small country gas station where the parking lot is hard packed dirt and they play music by Waylon and Willie and the boys. Don't call me because I don't have my cell phone with me, just chewing tobaccy, Mr. Samuel Colt, a thick roll of twenties, spurs that jingle, and a dog named Yeller. Well, mainly I have Visa, my health insurance card and allergy meds.

Robert Louis Stevenson once said, "For my part, I travel not to go anywhere, but to go. I travel for travel's sake. The great affair is to move." Stevenson would have loved a motorcycle.

Father's Day has been bought and purchased just like Christmas, and I've decided I'm not buying into it. I've got enough cologne to make even Congress smell good, and I have enough neckties — I only need about two — for making arm slings or tourniquets for snake bites. So it's just me, the motorcycle, and the open road.

You see things on a motorcycle unlike anything viewed from a car. In a car you sit in a compartment and even though you don't realize it, you see everything as though it was on TV. The scenes are all framed with no smell and no real sense of dimension while you sit still watching images go by. It's like trying to watch life on an old 35 mm movie film.

But on a motorcycle you are part of the scene. The asphalt whizzing by six inches below your boot is what you were walking on five minutes earlier, and it's now so blurred you can't focus on the small rocks and cracks that make up the road — yet you could put your foot down and touch it at any moment.

When you ride a motorcycle you converse only with your thoughts and hour after hour a man has plenty of time to ponder his sins and decide which ones to repent of and which ones might need a little more time to bake before they're done. You women do not need to do this because you are better than us men. Men know this.

As a father I've hit plenty of fouls and few homeruns. Mothers have the best batting score.

So I'm taking me and my sins and heading west. I'll join up with other fathers camping by a creek bank and sit by a crackling fire at night and share stories. It will be good to be with people that know the same songs I do such as "Me and Bobby McGee" and "I'll Fly Away" and "Big Rock Candy Mountain." We'll sing about being lonesome and about rivers gone dry. Come morning we'll pack up and ride through small towns without stopping and pass people in their cars, people sitting on their porches, and I'll see the envy on their faces. The journey is its own reward — revel in the freedom. Let no one tell you what to do.

But don't worry, I'll be back on Monday. I have a dental appointment.

Be Pleasant, Be Sweet, Be Southern!

I recently asked a friend to critique a presentation I gave and she said, "You seemed excited, nervous — borderline panic."

I said to her "The crowd was getting restless, I was losing them so I went for *enthusiasm*."

"Oh," she said.

I have been misunderstood a lot in my life and at times, so have you. You can't expect everyone to change his or her schedule and try to understand you. People are busy. I have learned however if you want to be understood then practice kindness and pleasantries, they are usually accepted at face value. I remember acts of kindness and pleasant comments said to me; they resonate a long time and become sweet memories.

Recently a security lady checked my ID at an airport and she said, "Have a great flight, Honey." Naturally this was in the South, the Charlotte Douglas International Airport to be exact. In the northern airports, a security woman would no more call you "Honey" than they would ask if you wanted to see their stretch marks. But as I walked down the concourse that "Honey" of hers kept flowing all over me. It was nice and I walked with a little spring in my step. I was a Honey. I've been called other names.

On the flight I sat next to a lady from Alabama who was a bit chatty. We fell into a conversation that turned to grandchildren. "I have six," she said and asked if I had any. I told her I had three, all girls, and they were the only perfect grandchildren in the world. I told her I was so sorry about hers, but there was only room in the world for three perfect grandchildren and they were mine. I would pray for her. She laughed at the humor. She patted my arm, wanted to know their ages, and the conversation went on like that for some time. When the flight ended and we were preparing to disembark, she said, "You take care of those perfect grandchildren, darlin'," and she patted my knee.

In other parts of the country, if a stranger touched you on the knee and called you darling you've got good grounds for a harassment lawsuit. But not in the South. We do and say nice things and think nothing of it. We're the ones that put ice in sweet tea, and it now appeals to both Baptist and Yankees (the heathen). We're like that, accommodating and nice.

I attended a business dinner while in New Orleans, and at the dinner I ran into a person I had not seen in ages. She threw her arms open wide and said, "Com'ere to me, boy!" and grabbed me in a bear hug that would have made an NFL linebacker wince. I think her perfume was Le Jack Daniels and lavender. Later as I worked the crowd I was honeyed, sunshined, sweetiepied, and occasionally I was cutie and sugar cheeks. The northern folks would smile, sip their Manhattans and say things like "merger" and "delicious shrimp."

We all want to be accepted and cool but we can't be. In high school I never made it to "popular" so I learned to settle for being pleasant and to accept such from other people out of respect. On my return to Charlotte I saw the same security woman and said, "Hello Honey, how are you?"

She smiled, winked and said, "Fine. Welcome back, Sweetie."

I grinned all the way to the taxi and thought how good it is to be pleasant — and so very Southern.

So ya'll be good now, Shuga. Ya heah?

5

Food

Big Decisions Are Best Made with Hot Dogs
Grilling Is a Southern Family Sport
It's Spring, Forget Politics and Think Banana Pudding
Baked Beans May Save the Family
We Need to Bake More Cakes
I Don't KitchenAid Anymore

Big Decisions Are Best Made with Hot Dogs

We are blessed community. We have a bit of joy and help here in times of recession, financial unrest, and lower back pain. This joy, this God sent wonder, this salve for the soul comes in the form of a food that can chase away trouble and anxiety. I speak, of course, of hot dogs. The mere mention of that American combination of bread, beef or pork wiener slathered in mustard, onions, chili — brings a peace to my spirit. Other places do not have the worlds' *best* hot dogs. We on the other hand, do. I say this humbly.

My city, Statesville, NC has several eateries that serve the *best* hot dogs in the world and First Pharmacy is the king of hot dog eateries.

A First Pharmacy hot dog is cooked just right, not rubbery or too soft, and the buns are perfect — not too much bread, not too little. The hot dog snaps as you bite into it and the flavor of meat, mustard, chili and onions mix together in your mouth, and you just know things are going to get better in your life.

The day was sunny and warm with blue skies filled with cottony clouds. I was with a friend and our lunch table was beside a big window. We watched the weather and saw people passing by on the sidewalk. An added enjoyment was friends that waved as they came in and went out, and you could see the traffic outside and all the while experience that incredible hot dog taste and texture. It was like sitting in a Norman Rockwell painting but with flavor.

While we ate, I listened to my friend who had a problem he had been dealing with for weeks. Today was a day of decision, hence the reason for these hot dogs — hot dogs induce wisdom. No matter how much haste you feel to dive into an issue, the hot dog holds a man back, you want to finish it first, and then tackle Armageddon. Many of our community's business people come here to discuss issues, and most eat more hotdogs than they tell their doctor.

The issue was serious and could be life changing. My friend was thinking of leaving our city. He had a chance to make more money in California. How could he turn down a little bit more? You're supposed to go where the money is, right? His business had grown and needed a bigger field in which to thrive. The decision made him uneasy; he could not get comfortable with it. He enjoyed his life here. This had become home. But business was, well, business.

We talked to each other around mouthfuls of delicious hot dog. The place was noisy with chairs scraping, people moving about, the sound of grease frying, and orders being called out across the room. Suddenly there came a squeal of "Grappa!" and a little girl ran up, bumped our table and put her arms out for my friend. I grabbed his drink before it could spill. He pulled her close and gave her a kiss on the forehead. Behind her was her mother, his daughter Lauren, smiling. Kindergarten had let out early today and a hot dog here at the Pharmacy was a treat from mom. The three talked a moment; Lauren had a funny sound in her car. Would her father check it sometime this week? Her husband, Jeff, was out of town. Of course her father would. He'd do it this afternoon. She thanked him, and mother and daughter left to go stand in line to order.

He watched them go, smiled, took a bite and remarked about how wonderful the hot dog was, that he had never had one so delicious as right here — how did they make them so good? He took another big bite.

His neighbor came by and asked if my friend was over his cold. There'd been a bad bug going around and did he know their friend

Big Decisions Are Best Made with Hot Dogs

Bill who worked at Lowes had come down with it. Bad stuff. After that his pastor and another acquaintance stopped to say hello.

"So," I said," for *a little bit more* you're tempted to rip up years of roots and move? This is a big decision my friend."

He grimaced.

Why is it we think satisfaction consists mainly of "more"? When do we get to enjoy the "more"? Like trying to find comfort at night, we twist and turn ever so slightly in search of a bit more comfort only to find we've lost what little we had and so we turn and toss, still seeking, hoping for satisfaction.

We both took big bites, savored the blend of onions, mustard and meat and nodded to someone waving to us from across the room. Lauren stopped by, holding a brown paper bag and said goodbye. "The girls" were headed to the park. They told him that they loved him.

We talked for a while longer, finished our meal and made our way outside. We stood on the sidewalk, and I turned to say goodbye. The sun was bright, you had to shield your eyes with one hand, cars passed, and people moved around us. My friend looked down at the ground and away from me, his hands in his pockets.

After a moment he slowly turned his head to face me and said with a soft grin, "I wonder if you can find hot dogs (he nodded to where we had sat, implying the whole experience) that good in California?"

"Nope," I replied, "you can only get that right here."

Grilling Is a Southern Family Sport

The slow hazy days of summer. Sweet corn is growing and it's okay to wear old worn shorts, battered Birkenstocks, and those T-shirts with pictures and slogans of restaurants, motorcycle companies and charity events.

Summer in our town is a time for grilling. We in the South call it "cookin' out." Grilling in the land of pickup trucks and shotguns is an important sport and an integral part of life. Marriages can dissolve over the proper way to grill chicken or barbeque ribs. My uncle Sid, a man who lived by his ability to deliver a perfectly cooked medium rare pork butt, was criticized by his wife one summer for sloppy use of seasoning and a weak smoke ring beneath the crust. They stopped speaking to each other. It was September before the tension broke bringing full reconciliation and the church threw a celebratory dinner. Their marriage counselor was so proud of them.

There was a time when grilling was a man-only sport but women have entered the arena of charcoal and gas. Grilling has become Pluribus Unum, yes ma'am.

It's a big deal.

Like many major events there is some etiquette and rules for grilling. This is important because we do not want to become careless lest we pick up bad habits and drift towards liberalism, which could lead us to plank salmon, portabella hamburgers, and stuffed pork chops with a blackened pâté. Southern grilling takes a conservative approach, just chicken, steak, and pork cooked in a way that assures a wholesome event and brings the entire family together.

To begin, first, center yourself. Become one with the back yard and the grill.

To approach a grill burdened with financial issues, worries about what the therapist implied about your love of pastels, worming the dog, your prostate report, etc. are just distractions and have no place in what you are about to do. Remember, you're playing with fire, literally. Therefore grilling etiquette is important, and always remember, that the first step can lead to success or failure.

Approach the grill calmly, not very fast but with a commanding determination. Stand before it and scratch your elbow or butt, spit to the side, do some stretches, and then slowly lift the lid. You now have "possession."

A rag dipped in cooking oil is then rubbed on the grill. This prevents sticking or "holding" and allows free movement or "traveling" of the meat you will be cooking. Light the grill and step back. You are practicing safety and projecting an image of confidence and control. Northerners, the uncouth, and maybe some Germans would simply throw a match in at this point and yell for beer. But not you. Stay focused.

Pick up the large tongs and fork hanging at the side of the grill and begin to talk loudly about how they should have been cleaned, does anybody work around here except you, and why do you have to do everything? This is called "outfield chatter" and you want lots of it. It lets you vent things you've had stored up inside of you all year and lets those around you know you have been industrious and simply did not have time to clean this and would a little help *kill* anybody?! The team needs to hear this.

Next place the meat on the grill thus putting it "into play."

Now get organized by complaining. This takes a bit of work but it brings everyone into the process. Call out for lemonade, a clean platter, where is the deck umbrella? You'll die in this heat — as if anybody cares. Glare at nothing in particular. Hint that the receiving of the lemonade is a bit slow today. This builds initiative in the family team, and they begin to pull together and overcome any remaining inertia. Now you've got everybody moving!

When the meat is cooked, bring it to the table on a big platter. Do this yourself as it establishes your image as a great coach, a Provider, the Giver of All Good Things. Place the meat in the center of the table or "bring it home." Go into a post game critique of the quality of the meat, the difficulties of grilling, and accept any thanks you may get for a job well done.

Then bow your head and thank God for propane, charcoal, good weather, and Maalox. Afterwards find a toothpick, settle back, review what you did, and make plans for the next game.

Go Team! Great job!

It's Spring, Forget Politics and Think Banana Pudding

I am not going to write about politics. I promised myself I would not do it — my doctor says I really should watch my blood pressure. Politics in a column is risky. Your verbs get shaky, your prose loses its rhythm and you start using phrases like "pre-emptive spin" and "fund balance transfer" and you become snippy and shoot words out in staccato bursts. It's pointless, you know why? Some things are going to continue on no matter what happens. I've seen flowers growing in a field that was burnt black just weeks ago. People in bomb ravaged Berlin built homes after World War II and had babies. The earth turns and for the billionth time, the seasons are changing.

Spring is here. I know because I checked that shady spot behind my shop and yep, the snow is finally gone. I'll let others complain about a cigarette smoking president and Congressional hacks exempting themselves from their own health care legislation. We have a national budget so unbalanced it may go out to a mall and shoot somebody.

If the North Pole melts I'll watch it on cable. The ocean will not come to Statesville and wash up to my front door and leave seaweed. Besides, none of my friends are Eskimos. If Iran makes a nuclear bomb they will use it first on Washington, which will really be a test for the new health care bill.

It's all buffalo chips to me.

I am going to sit in the shade and read sonnets and wait for a barren dogwood tree in my back yard to explode into glorious white petals. I imagine a float in a parade decorated with those white petals — the float moving just ahead of a marching band playing a John Philip Sousa march and popcorn and hotdogs being sold on the sidewalk and feel the pounding of the bass drum as it goes by where I'm standing in the crowd and everybody is laughing and having a good time. The sky is blue, the sun is shining, and to hear patriotic marches simply puts a tingle in your spine and a lump in your throat.

I just got all that from a bare tree.

Besides, the people that are going to pay for this current administration are under twenty-five years of age and they, like, have headphones in their ears — sweet — and like, you know, they can't hear what is going on around them. They have, like, 7,000 songs on their iPod, have not read Dickens (wassup with him?), and if you say "three trillion dollar deficit" they say, way awesome Dude — that on YouTube?

Whatever. Chill.

National politics is slop and for right now we should let the political pigs eat it. There is no new thing under the sun, so says the Bible. So we know that nations may crumble and fall but people will continue to fall in love and grandchildren will be born and our neighbors across the street will look after our house when we go on vacation.

A young woman will wait for her lover in front of the restaurant and when he walks into view she will smile, walk up to him, and kiss him on the cheek. They will hold hands and go inside to find a table. Her world will be filled with white dogwood petals and later they will have a house and children and so the world spins and so things go.

Let's take a day off from politics and let Congress fiddle while the economy burns. Find someone you love, take her hand, and

It's Spring, Forget Politics and Think Banana Pudding

tell her that her banana pudding is to die for. Then be still and enjoy being alive to experience spring. Because, you know dude, that is pretty awesome.

Later, we can vote.

Baked Beans May Save the Family

If we don't cook our own beans we may lose the family.

I realized this while I was attending an informal gathering. You know, the kind that starts out when someone you know believes they've been moved by a need to see more of everyone so you gather at that person's house, bring food, and take a shot at conversation.

I was looking at all the "homemade" food that was brought in and noticed most of it came in plastic containers with bar codes stuck on them revealing the fact that the contents were just passing through our area on a truck, like a stranger or a serial killer. The food had been mass-produced by a machine somewhere by someone someplace else. As my mother use to say, "Don't touch that, you don't know where it's been."

I wanted to say to the person that set a deli purchased container of baked beans on the table, "What, you didn't have time to actually bake a bowl of beans? It takes maybe thirty minutes and a little effort. Would it have killed you?"

I could just imagine the response: "My Blackberry went on the fritz, my attention deficient disorder was really acting up, our pet's therapist had to move the appointment, and my job keeps me really busy. My life is a struggle. I'm just lucky to be here."

Oh.

We're falling in love with self-importance and convenience and losing our way in the process. As a result homemade baked beans and families are headed for the endangered list along with the polar bear and the green sea turtle.

What if Jonas Salk, the man that made the polio vaccine possible, had decided to skip all that research because it was not convenient — he was so busy, and instead Googled around, got side tracked looking at cheaper ways to transport medicine and then got sidetracked again reading about a quick way to package aspirin in a bright colored box. Meanwhile we drop from polio.

Recently a friend told me she was so self-absorbed in her work that she did not even listen to her own children talking to her until the kids called her on it. They had to stand in front of her and wave their arms to get her attention. With a start she realized she had not heard a word that had been spoken (why were their arms waving?) but was sitting in the room totally focused on a career issue, staring into space. Embarrassed, she admitted their complaint was justified.

More and more our self-importance demands expediency that justifies convenience as we rush through the day en mass like lemmings, mindless to life, and to those we care about.

We speed dial the pizza delivery people and the family rushes to the table like water buffalo around a creek, eat fast then stampede to the next important thing on our schedule.

Meanwhile it's soothing and therapeutic to find a recipe, read it, and let it lead you gently along. A certain peace descends upon a house by the simple act of cooking — put a dollop of mustard, a bit of molasses and chopped onions into a bowl with some beans, mix well and you have the makings of home. The oven is hot and the baking dish has to be filled and stirred just right so that every bean and ingredient gets its fair share of the heat. You do this yourself, not virtually, not by email, but you make this dish with your own hands. Then gradually the kitchen fills with heavy savory smells — time slows down. You simply can't rush a good bean.

The process gives you time to ask someone how their day went and then to really listen to what they have to say, to check your kid's Facebook page and SAT scores, and while you wipe your hands on a towel you can reach over and give someone a quick kiss on the cheek. Just try to get that out of a plastic container.

If we don't take the time to bake the beans, the family's cooked.

We Need to Bake More Cakes

I walked into my office one day and found a fresh chocolate pound cake on my desk. The cake was perched on top of papers, notebooks, reports, sticky notes, and pencils (those are things that do not have software problems) scattered across the desk.

I've always assumed my desk was made of wood, but it would take big burly men with hard hats and bright yellow safety vests operating jack hammers to dig through the paper and junk to confirm there is wood down there. I am thankful the cake did not become lost amidst the clutter to be found centuries from now by archeologists on a TV documentary called *Food of the Ancients*.

The cake was wrapped in clear cellophane, had a white envelope on top with a handwritten note wishing me a happy birthday. The cake was from a co-worker, Margaret, who had taken the time.

This cake meant that recently in a kitchen bowls were brought out from shelves, eggs were broken, and flour was sifted and measured, spoons, spatulas and other tools were used and scattered about. Dishes were washed; others were used again. Upper cabinet doors were opened by reaching up on tiptoes and then the big bowl was taken out carefully so as not to drop it. Various drawers and boxes were opened and closed. The kitchen slowly became a mess.

Probably the phone rang while she worked and she had to answer it with her one clean hand and while pressing the phone to her ear with her shoulder she used both hands to measure vanilla extract as she told the caller what she was doing.

"…but that's all right. Ok…I'll talk to you later — uh huh…love you, too. Bye."

She poured the batter into a bunt cake pan, slid it into the oven and while the cake baked spent the rest of the afternoon cleaning up flour, eggshells, utensils, and drops of wet batter while planning supper for her husband.

Margaret and I are from a generation never divided and separated from each other by headphones, sealed cars, and the Internet. We learned to talk to people directly and shake hands or hug one another, and we covered our mouths when we coughed. We learned that we were not alone in the world — there are other people to be considered. My generation steps back every now and then, gets off the Internet, and bakes someone a cake.

The cake was handmade kindness to help ease the passing of time. At my age, birthdays are timely warnings as I become more aware of my decline and decrepitude. When someone tells me "You look great!" his or her eyes say, "For a guy your age." As you age, forward motion is a sign of good health especially if you can do it all upright and straight. I always try to keep enough momentum to reach the top of the next hill. Age also brings unease and concern about any dark cloudy spots on your CT scans. Colonoscopy results are special events.

Laboring for another person makes for good health and peace of mind. The current generation thinks life is about treadmills, texting, and blogs. But what we all want is a sense of worth and calling in life, and if we slow down enough, we may find it right in front of our noses. Labor can be its own reward.

Right now I am watching an electrician work on a fuse box in my house, and it is obvious that he loves his work. There is nothing like enthusiasm for what you do and there is no better satisfaction than to labor for another. Our Savior said that because He cares, He has worked to prepare a place for us. Not for himself.

I would not be surprised if when I meet Him at that place He has prepared, and I am welcomed in, He smiles, and offers me a freshly baked pound cake.

I Don't KitchenAid Anymore

The wonder of gourmet cooking and fine dining has left me. I knew this the moment I was sitting in a five-star Italian restaurant and realized I wanted a hot dog and fries. Not gourmet hot dogs imported from Italy mind you, but the wieners you find on sale at Food Lion and the frozen crinkle cut fries from Ore-Ida. I wanted the kind you used to get in pool halls and corner drug stores.

We have dozens of cookbooks in our kitchen — James Beard, Graham Kerr, First Baptist Church Cookbook of Favorite Recipes, and Betty Crocker Vol. 1 — all leftovers from the early 90s when men grew bored with space exploration and elephant hunting and realized you could socially rise above other men by using graters, recipes, and KitchenAid mixers.

In those days men compiled stock portfolios, smoked imported cigars, talked about their feelings, began eating salads and therefore were ultimately drawn to pastels. From there it was as short leap for everybody to start writing a book or interpreting art so in the natural course of things men discovered bouillabaisse and saffron.

When I was young and single I had a Peterbilt food processor and carried a Smith & Wesson nine millimeter diesel driven nutmeg grater in a kangaroo leather holster (you had to have a concealed permit for it). The kitchen became an extension of myself and I spent hours experimenting with marmalades and basil sausage vinaigrettes infused with African blackberry oil all tossed using ratchet wrenches — and Voila! — women swooned. Most men could not boil an egg and there I was, Master of Infused Oils, pouring timid but complex cabernet sauvignons and yammering about poached quail eggs while careful to voice concern about global warming and as an added plus, leave the toilet seat the way I found it. A man that could poach, had inner feelings *and* understood bathroom etiquette! Women slipped me their phone numbers on napkins.

In those days I shopped only at Williams-Sonoma and kept thirty-seven types of paprika and stored a small amount of specially produced bay leaves from Uganda in my gun safe. I was intense and would brook no insinuations about the virginity of my olive oils — I'd back it up with a fistfight or a shotgun. I once scoffed at a man's untidy arugula salad (his parmigiano shavings were too thick), and he broke into tears and came at me with a potato peeler. We grappled and rolled around in the floor until we had to stop to tend to our soufflés. We started to share our concerns about society's acceptance of frozen foods which led to a discussion of our childhood upbringing and the fact that we both had emotionally distant fathers and then the tears started flowing and we hugged each other. Now we're best buds and ride motorcycles together.

And then there was the time in Laredo I spied a young cowboy wrapped up in white linen, wrapped in white linen as cold as the clay. He'd accused a man of using thyme in a spaghetti sauce, but he was wrong. Alas poor Yorick, I knew him.

Then one day it ended. I served ten dinner guests Chilean sea bass with a chocolate risotto, and they claimed they'd never eaten anything so wonderful in all their lives and wept, they were overcome with joy. I realized I'd reached the pinnacle of cooking. I no longer needed to make the best crème d'spam or peanut butter gazpacho. I dropped my plutonium whisks and left the building. That part of my life was over. I've never looked back.

Now at Christmas I serve processed turkey or frozen ham with mash potatoes, yams and cranberries that all comes in a plastic tray covered with a thin plastic sheet that you microwave. Dessert is Twinkies right out of the package — accompanied with cold Red Bull right in the cans.

Our Lord said that He came that our joy might be full. He meant we should enjoy life and He did not obsess about soufflés.

It's not about food, it's about life. So get out there Honey Bunch, enjoy the sunshine and grill yourself an old fashion hot dog:

Hot Dog Recipe

One hot dog bun
One cheapo hot dog, cooked
Ketchup and mustard
Onions, chopped

Eat with a friend or while reading the latest spin-off of *The DaVinci Code*

6

Marriage and Other Daily Experiences

February and Hot Flashes Can Freeze a Man
Ferdinand Magellan and Me
What is Life All About?
Arresting Thoughts While Driving
All You Need Is Love at High Volume
Local Man Seeks Solitude, Claims to Be Normal
Life Is Unfair and the Trash Has to Be Taken Out
Let's Joke Around

I Saw a Real Parent at Burger King
The High Price of Togetherness
Her Boots Are the First to Hit the Ground
You Can Get It Together at the Stoplight
Draw On Your Ear and Sing Like a Viking
Domesticated Caveman Fuzzy on the Details
Doctor, I'm Tired of Pulling the Plow
Becoming a Cowboy — the Nu-Way
The Diet of a Pharisee
The Day My Barber Left Town

February and Hot Flashes Can Freeze a Man

February is a time of testing. The skies seem to stay dark — like God redecorated and ordered a gunmetal gray theme. We bundle up and listen to the wind outside shrill against the eaves and hope there is enough salt pork and flour to see us through to the spring.

Lucky me, I married Louise — Warrior Queen of the North. My wife has recently become as hot natured as a boiling cauldron. Icicles hang from the kitchen cabinets, the dog is frozen in place with one paw pointed up towards the thermostat, and she says, "Is it just me or is it hot in here?" She steps over a penguin to lower the temperature — again. Outside it's so cold squirrels are throwing themselves on electric fences.

I do not argue with the Queen. I go outside in 21-degree weather and walk around a bit without a coat and when I return back inside I feel warmer. There is cold and there is less cold. Sometimes you just need perspective.

Luckily, I grew up on a farm where you accepted winter the way you accept your looks — with resignation. Nothing you can do about it really.

There were no TV weather forecasts for people on the farm, just a sudden sense of doom, and old people saying their bones ached while we inventoried the jars of canned beans, corn, and okra. As far as meat, they said that God would provide. A family of ten would be reduced to a group of eight by spring and everyone would appear well fed — there were never legal inquiries.

Winter on our hog farm was intense and gave you a shot of determination. Can you survive? Yes, if you really want to.

So with jaw set you trudge outside to do chores at six in the morning while the air still has the sharp bite of the cold night and the sun has yet to rise and give you hope. My job was to take a hammer to the water troughs and break what had frozen over night so the hogs could drink. The big swine would stand in the unheated shelters looking at me. I remember one very gentlemanly Berkshire boar hog, his eyes staring at me with icicles hanging from his snout. His eyes seem to say "Kill me now. Please." I swung the hammer and hit the trough of ice instead and you could just see the disappointment on his face.

My father thrived on adversity and winter was his special challenge. If he could not see your breath while you worked outside then he called the whole thing off until the temperature dropped a bit more. He would put on long johns, two pairs of pants, a heavy flannel shirt, winter coat, gloves, hat, and then go outside to supervise my work. He would stand bundled up and watch me clean pens, repair broken gates, and slats with my hands numb from the cold and say "Winters just don't get cold like they used to."

Days of old fashion farming, cows with names like Clarabelle, and beloved old mule teams are a thing of the past. So, like our parents who reminded us that they walked ten miles to school in the snow and twenty miles back, I had to tell this story.

I'm sitting here freezing, trying to write this column while my wife wonders if we should take the quilts off the bed. Menopause is a mystery I intend to ask God about first thing when I see Him. But right now, I'm thinking of crawling in our freezer to keep warm.

Ferdinand Magellan and Me

When I was in the fourth grade I could read faster than everyone else and so my order for Scholastic books was bigger than any other kid in my grade. So much reading resulted in a need for glasses and then I became pensive, expanded my vocabulary, and began to take clarinet lessons. My classmates took that to mean that I was intelligent, but nowadays they would call me a nerd or a geek.

Kathy Emerson, the blond class beauty, had a problem with her history homework and just before we had to turn it in one morning she asked me, "What did that guy Magellan do?" I gave her the answer in time for her to scribble it on her homework paper. She then told everybody that I had brains and I was labeled: "Smart."

Labeling can be misleading. What they did not know was that I had an uncle in the 11th grade in high school and at nights I just called him on the phone and gave him my homework questions and voila! I got the answers. This prepared me for the administrative work I now do. You don't have to know everything, just how to find answers and solutions before the paperwork is due.

Kathy liked the guys that were athletic, so I wrote a song about being an athlete. I called it "The Athlete." At some point I was hoping to hook up with the Beatles — or Kathy. But when I played the song at the Monday morning "What I did over the weekend" presentation and dedicated it to her, I got the living daylights beaten out of me at recess by Tom Quiggins. How was I to know that Tom liked Kathy — a lot? The façade of being smart was paper-thin and brains could not outrun muscle.

    I started to resent the fact that now I was always supposed to have all the answers — my label was a burden. I wanted to astonish everyone by jumping outside of my label, which I did and landed directly into sports — playground football to be exact. Nobody expected me to catch the ball that Cletus Jackson threw at me, but I did. It surprised me so much that I stood there grinning, which was a mistake. I was tackled and someone yelled, "Pile on!" and I became the foundation of a human pyramid. It took a week to get all the dirt out of my mouth and nose. I learned to shy away from glory.

    As I grew up I encountered other labels — " guitar player," " graduate," and one day it became "father." I'm older now and accept labels; it's part of life. Due to my age the AARP recently labeled me Knowledgeably Mature, which is crazy because I misplace my wallet, which then distracts me so that I am late for my doctor's appointment. And don't get me started on "did you take all your pills today?" because I have no idea — that is why they have emergency rooms! I walk a treadmill while listening to my iPod; a man caught between two worlds — a health geezer.

    Labels like "neighbor," "motorcycle rider," "friend," and "dad" are kind of nice. I accept them all along with my stomach meds and do not make a fuss. In fact, I'm beginning to pity young people; they have so much label transitioning ahead of them. I've put in my time so call me what you will but at this stage in life — I'm just "me."

    And to think I arrived at this point in life, and was able to write this story, all because Kathy Emerson had no idea that Ferdinand Magellan was the first to sail around the world.

What is life all about?

If recent events were not so awful, their frequency of occurrence would make them boring. The morning headlines scream at you, each one so terrible you shake your head in disbelief and begin reading sentence after sentence of horror — your forgotten coffee and Danish grow bitter and cold.

The list is frightening: Massive killings in schools by self-centered crazies. An ex-cop declares war on law enforcement officers and dies in a fiery shoot out. Guns are issued in schools for the protection of teachers and students, and disgruntled people go on random shooting sprees in California (of all places).

It seems that anyone who has not gotten their own way goes on a rampage or throws a hissy fit with a loaded weapon. Is there a gas leak?

One has to wonder what is happening to us. We, like sheep, have gone astray and need a good sedative. The noise of bullets, murders, killings, riots, wars, terrorist's acts and the yammer of political leaders are so loud you can barely hear yourself think. We are so busy grabbing and talking about our own wants and needs that we've lost sight of the purpose for our lives.

The meaning of life was a big topic in the 1960's when people with long hair and bell bottom pants smoked hallucinogens and attended Pete Seeger concerts. Volkswagen minivans painted with rainbows and flowers carried thousands to live concerts where folk groups told us where all the flowers had gone and the answers were blowing in the wind. Then they signed big recording contracts.

And still the question remains, what is life all about?

Simple — to know God and to serve Him.

It's a clear truth but like the nose on your face the evidence is so close it can make your eyes cross if you focus on it too hard. It will take a little faith to see us through and what else but faith in a loving God can keep you afloat in such corrupt and violent times? When a society stops looking up and stares at the ground for support it begins to die as a civilization.

As the country temporarily goes to the dogs, cats must learn to duck and dodge and to be wise and vigilant. They must walk on fence tops, sleep in tall trees and have faith that all this barking and growling will not become a way of life forever. For everything there is a time and it's time cats kept quiet, remain beautiful and wait for daylight.

Self-righteousness, greed and corruption are cruel taskmasters when they take the helm, and neither legislation nor the Gospel will stay their cold evil hands.

The bell bottomed long haired hopes for changing the world never gained enough altitude to clear the trees and now we've become the very people we use to snicker at — the old and cautious, but thankfully, there is still faith.

Faith still lives due to the endurance of gentleness and the ability to laugh. Gentleness is found all around us in daily life and faith reigns through the ordinary: through conversations in driveways, through tending pets, gardens and picking fresh tomatoes, through sports, anticipating the spring, making love, sharing French fries, holding new born babies — all places where the sweet molasses mixes with grace and love and makes for good sopping.

Though we live in a time of gargantuan greed and vanity, one can look a short distance every evening and see the porch lights of gentle people, our neighbors. Are we our brother's keeper?

What is life all about?

The answer is yes, and therefore we should love each other and every once in a while sneak up from behind and give that person a good wedgy.

Arresting Thoughts While Driving

I'm riding down Interstate 40 thinking about my tennis elbow and Obamacare — which led me to worry about national bankruptcy. And how will we eat when the army locks all the food in secured warehouses and that in turn made me think about something for supper — then there was a blue light flashing behind me. One minute you're part of the regular crowd, an honest person headed home thinking about pizza delivery and mobs in the streets; the next minute you're pulling over onto the highway's Shoulder of Shame. You wonder if the night will end with you wearing a bright orange jumpsuit and being served bread-and-water in lockup.

You try to be upbeat — maybe the jail will have some nice Italian bread with herbs and a balsamic dip. Maybe your cellmate will be a timid drunk named Dwayne rather than a very lonely muscular man called "Bull."

Your first thought is to not act in a suspicious manner. Law enforcement officers hate it when you act in a suspicious manner. The officers become cautious and may suspect they are dealing with a criminal or a Washington lobbyist — two species that you always approach with caution.

If at that moment a rabid badger bursts into your car and dives into your lap you must ignore it completely or they'll think your frantic activity is an attempt to conceal something. So never mention the badger. These are trained professionals, and they are not fooled by Sudden Badger Syndrome. Just lean over, put both hands out the driver's window, and act like the guilty scum that you are.

Things go through your mind. You promise God anything if He'll get you out of this. Or you hope the trooper just became a missionary, and he'll start practicing grace and forgiveness right now before he goes to Rwanda. You'd make a great first test case.

Suddenly you remember that time in 1974 when you were dancing in a crowd of people in Atlanta at Ruby's Red Warehouse. You pulled a yellow lever marked "Do Not Pull." Who knew the building's fire suppression system would work so well — and that polyester bell-bottom suits retained so much water? A little spontaneous fun seemed like such a neat thing to do at the time. Now, after all these years, they've finally found you and you're going to be the poster child for Cold Cases Solved.

Your heart pounds as your tires touch the rough shoulder of the road. You cling to hope, maybe it's a forgotten parking ticket but deep down you think — what if he has a warrant and you're going to get a matching set of ankle bracelets? You wore sneakers today, you should have worn loafers. On TV they remove your shoelaces and belt. You realize you'll have to walk with your toes curled to keep your shoes on.

The blue light is beside me but then continues on. What's this? The officer passes me — he was after someone else. You accelerate back onto the road as relief washes over you. It feels wonderful to be out from under judgment, a good lesson to remember — obey the law. But then human nature regains control and relief is replaced with smugness and you smote your breast and thank God you are not as other men are — liars, extortionists, publicans, or speeding motorists.

Now I'm steering with my knees and typing all of this into my Blackberry.

You say what?

Yeah, I know you're not suppose to text in a car but this is just for a second…and the knees…aw, c'mon, geeez! It's not like I'm a liar or an extortionist or a publican or…

All You Need is Love at High Volume

After all these years I had no idea that Beatles John Lennon and Paul McCartney could help me get through a stop light.

The day was absolutely beautiful as I pulled up to a major intersection with my windows down taking in the smells and warmth of a spring day.

All at once I heard the "wump, thud, wump, wump" sound of musical bass from the car beside me. The driver had his windows down and his sound system was playing music, which consisted of words with no melody all playing loud enough to shatter concrete. Imagine kicking over a trash can and screaming — that sounds better than what I heard. My pickup truck began to shake, and I thought I could feel the tartar falling off of my teeth.

I am bothered by those who play their music so loud that the rest of the world is forced to listen to it. It reminds me of my age.

I looked at the small car with its patchy paint job and then at the driver, who was slumped way down in the seat wearing a baseball cap pulled low over his forehead. I started to say something to this rude kid but then I had an idea.

I could challenge him on his own turf. We could have a musical shootout right here. Both of us may go away hearing-impaired, but my manly man indignation was riled and demanded satisfaction. Ladies, it's a guy thing.

I checked my console to see what kind of ammo I was shooting today. I saw some classical *Vivaldi — Spring, Tom T. Hall's Greatest Hits, Jimmy Buffet Live in Concert* and, AHA! *The Beatles' Greatest Hits!*

I put the Beatle CD into my player and programmed it for "She Loves You" and spun my volume control like a roulette wheel. Ringo's opening drum roll from highs to the low bass drum came out loud and strong. My hair blew back as though a great wind had just blown through my truck cab. The paper and trash on the floor of the truck bounced into the air, and the speaker grills rattled in the doors. I looked over at Ball Cap Guy but he showed no signs of being aware I existed. Perhaps brain dead?

I turned the volume up even higher, probably interfering with NASA's attempt to contact aliens and then, at long last, Mr. Ball Cap sat up. He turned his head toward me and stared, dark sunglasses under the brim of a hat. He lowered his volume just as Paul and John were singing "With a love like that, you know you should be glaaaad!"

I started moving my hands about, shaking my shoulders, and rolling my head back and forth as if I was in music ecstasy or maybe had sat on a nail.

I looked at him and pointed my thumb at my chest as if to say, "This is my music, got a problem?" But instead of reacting rudely or shrugging me off, he sat up, grinned, and gave me a thumbs-up nodding his head in approval. I yelled at him "The Beatles!" He gave me a slow nod, another thumbs-up, and mouthed, "Nice."

We sat there, two guys at an intersection listening to John and Paul taking leads and harmonies and singing about simple love and romance. He was no longer an inconsiderate jerk — he was actually a lost musical soul in need of guidance.

The light changed and he went on his way leaving me bewildered at his reaction. Who knows, next time he pulls up beside me he may be playing "All You Need is Love."

As for me I'll stop judging, keep a cleaner truck, and play a little music.

Lennon and McCartney would be so proud.

Local Man Seeks Solitude, Claims to Be Normal

Thankfully it was over. The week had been a marathon of speaking to different groups about various issues such as my column (Mr. Hudson, does all that stuff really happen?), managerial challenges, and budget constraints. I even traveled across the state and spoke about my day job with the city — which is my cash crop — so I put all the zing I had into "Project Management, Administration and Good Luck." It was a spiel that compared public finances to bowel disorders — they laughed. They said I would be invited back.

All week I shook hands, ate out of Styrofoam containers, returned phone calls on the run, and arrived home to find a boatload of people in my house — kids, adults, and teenagers. These people were my grandkids, neighbors, and immediate family — but still, I had enjoyed all the human contact I could stand for one week.

As I headed upstairs to unpack, the wispy fog that serves as my brain began to form a thought which coalesced into one declarative sentence without enhancing modifiers: I want to be alone.

Now before you label me anti-social ask yourself — is wanting to be alone a bad thing? Ah, Grasshopper, it is not.

Big Decisions Are Best Made with Hotdogs

Long bearded hermits who do not use hair conditioner or deodorant sit alone in secluded mountain caves and no one talks smack about those guys. Being alone does not mean I want to sit in a room and make a bomb or write country songs about momma gettin' run over by a train or that I need a good cry. Superman had his Fortress of Solitude and the Bible tells us Jesus left the multitude and went into the mountains to be alone. He needed some away time, cleared his calendar, and bolted for the hills. The disciples took messages, made notes, and juggled the work schedule until He came back. No big deal.

I love to connect with people, and I love to disconnect with people. I like winter/summer, hot/cold, folk/classic, night/morning, Obama/Palin. Differences and opposites spice up our lives and solitude is just another seasoning in life's great stew.

Men are sometimes seized by an urge to climb a tall tree, hang from a branch by one hand, and use the other to scratch their stomachs and check out things below. It's quiet up there; the leaves rustle in the wind and for a moment we are above our problems. We sniff and feel around for some easy fruit to munch on — find a nice branch, sit on it, and gaze into nothing.

When our son was small sometimes we would be away from home for two or three days and upon our return, he would race upstairs, close the door to his room, and stay there for hours. I would sneak up to the door and listen to him talk to himself. He scripted adventures and instructed the toys as to what they were suppose to do. He was alone — happy as a bullfrog with both legs.

It is important in a marriage that each partner gives their spouse some "alone" time. Seasoned marriage partners accept the fact that from time to time we all need to sit, stare into space, and allow the drool to run down our chin. Don't ask, don't tell. It has nothing to do with love — it's about shell shock.

Sitting here upstairs at my desk just now I heard a child squeal which made the adults go into hysterical laughter; the phone rang, the dog started barking, and I heard something go bump and then there was a crash. I am going to softly close my door now.

See you later. 'Bye.

Life Is Unfair and the Trash Has to Be Taken Out

Jon and Kate Gosselin of the now defunct show *Jon & Kate Plus 8* had experienced nothing that has not happened to thousands of other couples — they got married, had kids, threw up their hands, and called the lawyers. However, the Gosselins pulled down boatloads of money for that mess.

The rest of us mop the kitchen floor, get the kids to school, and make sure the dog has water — all without the big bucks. The righteous suffer and Gosselinites prosper. Life is not fair; we all know this.

I grew up in a house with only one bathroom and two sisters; I know something about unfairness and suffering. Most mornings I needed some alone time, but the bathroom door would inevitably be closed. I would bang on the door as I hopped from one foot to the other trying to avoid sudden relief, and my Mother would tell me that was rude, to wait my turn. Mornings at our house could be tense.

One day Mother tried Socialism. She called us into the kitchen and pointed out that we all had five minutes each for only one bathroom; the bathroom belongs to the people, not an individual. Her eyes were wide and crazed, and she waved a big spatula in the air adding that we would all learn to love one another and live like Christians, even if it killed us.

Big Decisions Are Best Made with Hotdogs

You push through childhood and yearn for the day people will treat you properly. You try to find it in college through academic performances like chemistry class as you explain how an equation showing the oxidation of sodium with air can be mathematically balanced — hoping to impress lovely Cathy who sits beside you in class. She has auburn hair, long legs, brown eyes, and full lips. This makes her the most wanted woman in the universe. After class one day you ask her out to the homecoming football game. She tells you, "I like you as a friend but no, I'm going with someone else. Thanks, you're so sweet." She walks out of your life.

This loss may cause you to switch from rock n' roll music to country songs like "I'm So Lonesome I Could Cry," "Tennessee Whiskey," and "Always On My Mind," and your heart bleeds by the gallon. You also consider medical treatment for your acne and consider membership in a good local gym.

Or maybe you get a job — work hard, be a team player, but other people are promoted. You instead get a heavier workload, then your furnace dies, your prostate enlarges, and your neighbor wins the lottery. You chafe against unfairness.

You reach a fork in life — become bitter or keep reaching out for new experiences: maybe try writing or chinchilla farming. You now know that either way there will be disappointments, as well as joy, and that the trash has to be taken out every day.

Remember unfairness has broadened your understanding. You can now feel for the masses of people that suffer unrequited love. You've been humbled and appreciate things you did not earn, like sunrise and your child's first words. You will never cut in line and take someone's rightful place. You know how that feels.

You bumped into unfairness but you lived through it. Some things you cannot change, you make peace with life and try to get more fiber in your diet.

Along the way you buy a house with two and half baths and have a family. Maybe you write a newspaper column or a book and people like it. You're glad you kept reaching out for new experiences.

If you learn that unfairness is something you have to reach over then you'll start to smile a lot, even when taking out the trash.

Let's Joke Around

I was amused lately when a man who owns a national company that sells chicken sandwiches answered a question regarding marriage, he thought it should be only between a man and a woman, and suddenly conservatives and liberals are hurling accusations at each other like javelins. Massive crowds gathered at the eateries to show support or condemnation, which created huge waiting lines. A few just wanted lunch.

These are Spanish Inquisition days where every statement is analyzed for the tiniest bit of potential offense. This is a sad fact in the country that gave the world Red Skelton, Jackie Gleason, Bill Cosby, Johnny Carson, and dozens of funny TV sitcoms. Now we've become a shrill, tense group of people glaring at each other with our arms folded across our chests. Cars, the Internet, and email all physically separate us; we hear our own voices too much. We don't joke anymore.

Back before we decided we were all oppressed there were two good ways to get to know a person. You could work beside someone doing an unpleasant job like cleaning up road kill or digging postholes and another way was to tell jokes — like the one about a horse that walks into a bar and just stands there. The bar tender looks at him and says, "Why the long face?"

I've heard that joke a million times and it still makes me smile. And there were good old "Knock Knock" jokes about Dexter and the halls and the one about Mr. Walter when the well runs dry. And of course there was the Buddhist that refused Novocain for his root canal because he wanted to transcend dental medication.

We use to laugh a lot. Then everybody got cell phones and there was no need to see each other.

Now, jokes are only told but up until the 1960s people use to play jokes. Cars and machines were simple. My father and his pals disassembled a neighbor's Farmall tractor and reassembled it in the man's tobacco barn. It took the farmer a day to find his tractor. Of course there was good-natured pay back later. Tying tiny bells to the bottom of a young married couple's box spring mattress always got a wink and a smile. Many homes, like your grandmothers', had outhouses that your friends tipped over at the most delicate moment. My friends did that to me one time and that's how I learned to cuss.

Telling a joke right has nothing to do with your political affiliation, religion, education, or income. You do not need physics or theology everyday, but the ability to tell a good joke always comes in handy. Some people develop a knack for it like making hoop shots with a swish.

Nobody knows where jokes come from. Years ago I was standing in the Charlotte Douglas Airport watching a news report on a big screen TV that was following up on a president that had sexual relations with a young intern. Standing beside me in a blue business suit was a gentleman I had never seen before. He turned to me and said, "Did you hear Belk is having a President's Day sale? All men's pants are half off!" He had heard a version of that joke in a New York diner.

Jokes help you release tension, even oldies like my favorite fifth grade joke, "Why do gorillas have large nostrils? Because they have big fingers." Or "The blind man picked up a hammer and saw."

Your life may be in a ditch, your in-laws are coming over for the weekend, and you've misplaced your car keys but a good joke every now and then will do you good. So tell a joke, give out a laugh, and let's all sit down and eat.

I Saw a Real Parent at Burger King

Years ago my son was born in the month of April — right on schedule. Getting a kid to hatch in sync with future school enrollment periods takes work and planning. The man must be injected with an oyster-Viagra solution three times a day. The woman must eat lasagna and hang upside down for two hours during a full moon. She then has to stand on her right foot with her left leg slightly bent extending both arms outward from her sides at shoulder height — the Stork Position — for 28.7 minutes. The man's performance is paced by a clock and temperature readings.

The baby was born due to the labor of my wife with me in the background begging the doctor for a sedative. I was totally ignored through the entire birthing process and had to make do with a lint covered M&M I found in my pocket.

My son is athletic with a dry sense of humor, which is a good thing. We Hudsons are in need of a humor gene carrier and now we seem to have one. He embraces life with an iPod, has many friends, and believes the sun comes up just for him. He is as healthy as a plow horse and at seventeen, believes fast food is best enjoyed without parents.

Moms and Dads work hard at building a kid. We lay a foundation to build on — like saying "Please" and "Thank You" and why you flush the toilet after you use it. At sixteen, we lecture them about what time to come home — and it's always a lot earlier than they think.

Anything happening at midnight is bad and anything past 2 a.m. is probably illegal. After midnight the good responsible people are asleep but by 2:30 a.m. an active person feels independent and may want to become a celebrity or a scuba diver — right then. Parents never discuss how we know this.

I saw the essence of parenting recently while standing in line at a local Burger King. The place was packed and the line very long. After a ten minute wait a woman with a twelve-year-old son finally made it to the cashier. She tried to order a hamburger for herself and a hamburger and large fries for her son. Her son began to complain in a slurred voice. I then noticed he had Down syndrome. He thought he was going to get a hotdog, which was unavailable, and he stomped away from her and sat down at a nearby table. He did not understand.

He stared down at the floor; his small shoulders slumped. He was slowly collapsing — his head sinking lower into his shoulders. When you are different than everyone else and the world ignores you, you hope for small things, and sometimes even those seem to be snatched from you at the last minute — after you've gotten to wish for it.

The mother left the cashier and walked over to her son. She cupped his face in both her hands and said something to him. She kissed his nose, tickled his stomach and he giggled. She then stood up straight, walked again to the back of the line, and with her hands I saw her wipe big wet tears from her eyes.

I was going to offer her my place but now her face was puffy, her mouth set hard by responsibility. I looked away. Sometimes parenting scrapes you raw and you need a moment.

I hope her husband gives her a kiss and a surprise tickle when he comes home so that she laughs, pulls away, playfully hits him on the shoulder, and hugs him tight. Her face will have a smile, her eyes will twinkle and for a little while she will be a parent with no tears.

The High Price of Togetherness

Fall and winter weather brings us indoors and corrals us like penned livestock at the county fair. This togetherness demands politeness which in turn, demands we interact, which allows the flu to move from runny noses to hearty handshakes and soon the entire herd is infected — sickened by good manners and the bonhomie of togetherness.

During flu season some years ago my family left to visit my wife's folks, and the boxer and I were left behind to keep the home fires burning. A few days earlier I had politely shaken about three hundred hands after speaking at a seminar on public health and drinking water. Now I planned a weekend of pizza, war movies, and more pizza. But I felt sick and achy.

By night I had fallen down the deep dark well of flu. I lay in bed drenched in sweat, my bedclothes damp and twisted around me. My joints were on fire and my head was a bass drum that beat with a vengeance. The world turned dark and miserable. I would drag myself out of bed to get things like ginger ale, saltine crackers, and more blankets. I lost track of time, what day it was, my street address, and the concept of America. I no longer cared about gas mileage or quick relief from hemorrhoids.

Big Decisions Are Best Made with Hotdogs

I was hot and felt like someone had hit me in the stomach with a baseball bat. I hurried to the toilet then returned to bed and collapsed on sheets that were pulled off the corners of the mattress. I burrowed into blankets that had become infused with sickness. My mouth tasted like I had eaten bad gopher meat.

I dozed off, then awakened, and was cold and there weren't enough blankets so I put on my old blue bathrobe. Still cold, I saw my wife's pink bathrobe and put that on — gender distinction was now one of many casualties. The fire inside me grew and I threw the robes and blankets off. My stomach would sink and then rise and I turned green.

I had short vivid snatches of dreams, sometimes running through a woods while something chased me. I would hop over rocks, dart around trees and yet always that "something" was behind me, chasing me, threatening to take my life. I vowed to have a greater appreciation for rabbits in the wild. The flu lasted two days and a night that blended into an eternity.

Finally I awoke and felt a bit better. The house was dark, chilled and quiet. I got up and went downstairs to the kitchen. I turned on the light switch. The clock on the wall showed the time to be 5 a.m.

The kitchen looked like the 82nd Airborne had passed through it! Saltine crackers were scattered all over the counter, cabinet doors had been thrown wide open, balled up tissues were strewn about, a liter of ginger ale with the top off had gone flat and sat by the sink. Red and white Tylenol capsules were scattered beside an empty water glass and an unbroken stream of paper towels ran from the towel rack on the counter down to a folded-over pile on the floor — evidence of a quick pull gone terribly wrong.

My gaze settled lower to the floor. A bottom cabinet door had been left open. The dog had found a box of Pop-Tarts and her belly was swollen as she licked up what looked like her thirty-seventh Pop-Tart. From the looks of the floor she had eaten her way through a buffet of Cheerios, all-purpose flour, marshmallows, a blue sponge, and something that was green. The fall of Rome was prettier than this.

I stared mouth open and wide-eyed at the scene. The dog stopped for a moment and looked up at me with an expression that said, "What?"

I snapped the lights off and went back to bed.

So beware. Handshakes, friendliness and close conversations, the very things that bring us together can send us spiraling out of control down the deep well of misery. Have a nice day.

Her Boots Are the First to Hit the Ground

My wife is a teacher, an elementary grade educator; her boots are the first to hit the ground in America's offensive to educate its young.

She arises at 5:30 each morning and is out the door and ready to receive busloads of second grade kids by 7 a.m. Many of these little bodies have not been fed, washed, or have clean clothes. They stumble bleary eyed into class, small bundles of life — some have already known abuse and some have homes that have the ambience of a late night bar during a brawl. Little angels bound to the ground.

She returns home and tells me about the forty pound kid that dumped a load in his pants, the parent that could not be reached at any phone number on file, the timid student teacher (you must stare the children down or all thirty will bolt for the bathroom like gazelles), the kid that dropped Mr. Snowball the hamster — cage and all — in the floor during quiet time, and the diva parent who expects the school system to raise her child and demands a conference for which the whining mother never shows up though teacher and principal waited a half hour past the appointed time. And I pour my wife a stiff diet Coke on ice that she tosses down her throat, places the glass down on the kitchen counter, and says, "Hit me again."

Public school teaching is a divine calling and comes with much frustration. Sometimes she grits her teeth. The heat in the building does not work, she got a new kid that does not speak English and neither do the parents, and she endures the ill-designed rating of schools that depend on a teacher's performance judged by the whim of a child.

Yet the teacher in her pushes on. Her complaints about pay are good-natured; she loves her job, is paid a fraction of what she is worth yet maintains a high level of professionalism.

Professionalism in education is a world apart from mine: mine requires no more than a computer key board, a cocky attitude, a bag of pork skins, and interesting underwear.

Three thoughts to all beleaguered teachers:

1. Remember, you are a professional. You are not a paper-pusher at Amalgamated Brooms. Before politicians began telling your profession how to teach, your predecessors built the framework for the world's greatest country — America. So stand tall.
2. Hang out with other teachers. Never chum around with principals or administrators. They have their own agendas and crosses to bear. You can be nice but not fawning or subservient. Don't gravitate there, they sometimes draw fire.
3. Do not passively accept ugly remarks or rude behavior from parents. Stand up and leave the room or simply hang up on them if it's a phone conversation. The problem in education is not lack of money, politicians (What!?), or global warming — it's bad parents. Spoiled, lazy parents are the enemy of education and when school boards find a legal way to treat them as such, these over indulged narcissists will be put in their place and the respect for your profession will return.

Maybe in a hundred years from now teachers will be treated like a holy priestly order akin to the Illuminati or the Order of

Melchizedek but in the mean time teachers will arise each day, wipe little noses, endure a myriad of naïve policies, yet somehow pour knowledge into an impressionable little mind. And one teacher will come home, gulp down a diet Coke on ice, and say to her husband, "They dropped Mr. Snowball today — cage and all."

You Can Get It Together at the Stoplight

The stoplight coming out of the Shoppes at Broad Street is one of the longest traffic lights in the world. I think there is one in Brazil that stays red longer, but folks down there do not care about traffic laws. Brazilian stoplights are mere decorations. Meanwhile, if I pull up to the Shoppes traffic light with my wife and son the mood becomes one of impatience.

"Dad! Why did you go out this way?" my son moans. "I graduate from college in four years — I'll be late!"

He writes "HELP ME" inside on the rear window of the car. People on the sidewalk begin to stare.

"Take the short cut," directs my wife. "I want to get home before the sun becomes a brown dwarf." (we're a big Discovery Channel family). She points to the right implying the short cut is that-a-way.

We take the short cut and drive through a parking lot, go behind a mall, cross a barren desert, plunge through a raging river, negotiate our way through a rainforest, hang a left behind a warehouse, and bounce back onto a paved road with a stoplight that is now more acceptable to my family. My darlings ride in sullen silence, staring out the window with their arms crossed.

Me, I like stoplights and the one at the Shoppes at Broad Street is my favorite.

Big Decisions Are Best Made with Hotdogs

A stoplight is a place of guilt free rest and would probably get the approval of our Puritanical-work-ethic ancestors. "Yea and when thou comest to the burning red light thou shalt apply thy brake and sit and be still and know that this is good and not evil. And the stoplight shall be a sign to you and your family, yea a sign of rest all the days of your life." A spiritual moment of cease and desist.

At a stoplight you get to do *nothing*.

While you wait for the light to change you are not expected to write memos, cut the yard, call the plumber, clip your toenails, email your mother, do your taxes, fold clothes, sweep the kitchen, call the dentist, write a speech, cook a hot meal, vacuum the house, nor fax, twitter, tweet or Google. It is legally appointed downtime and way too short if you ask me.

You spend your day driven by pressure (work) and everybody else's schedule (kids, soccer, kids, dance lessons, kids, kids, kids, etc.). You zoom across town to pick someone up just in time to zoom by the bank and zoom to pick up clothes at the cleaners and zoom to the drugstore. It's like living with an outboard motor strapped to your back.

You race through the city at least eight miles per hour over the legal speed limit (Oh get over it — you know you do it) and your breath is coming in gasps — when suddenly a red traffic light appears, you slow down and stop. The cycle of madness is temporarily halted by order of the state.

You settle down and begin to breathe normally and your hands release their death grip from the steering wheel. You notice the sun is out, the sky is blue, and birds fly by. You realize once again that you love your family and the fantasy of running away to a commune in Peru where only sundials show the passing of time was just a stress-induced idea. At a stoplight you can get your bearings. You remember your name.

So if you see me sitting beside you at a traffic light with a dazed smile — let me be. I'm having a ball doing nothing. And it's legal.

Draw On Your Ear and Sing Like a Viking

Recently my mind took a short vacation and went to Cancun or Myrtle Beach or somewhere and left me sitting in Starbucks reading a story I had written on a napkin. The top of my ear began to itch, and I absentmindedly scratched it with a ballpoint pen. A minute later I realized I had drawn all over my ear and cheek. A quick glance into a nearby mirror showed I had sketched a rough draft of South America — or maybe the digestive system of a parrot.

I felt my face turn red, and I noticed an attractive woman walking my way. She stopped, placed a clean napkin on the table, and said, "I've never seen anybody do that before. Never." I did not take that as a compliment. The very next day I slipped off a curb and with arms waving in the air I over compensated and crashed backwards onto the asphalt. A passing lady stopped, looked down at me, and, just as her mother had taught her regarding people lying in public streets, she asked, "Are you all right?"

"Yes," I said. "I'm okay. Thank you very much."

And I am okay too, really. The pen and ear incident was due to inattention and so was the ungraceful fall, but once winter sets in and autumn is done with all its drama, emotional upheavals and lost opportunities to lose weight before the holidays and we start wearing heavy coats and anticipate the first snow — then we will recover our sense of balance and we'll focus on survival instead of scribbling on ourselves and falling about.

I know people who are hoping for some more clear 70 degree Saturdays for leaf raking but it's not going to happen. God has moved on. Most of us have raked our yards and are pumped up about the coming snows. We're like a chorus of Nordic villagers coming on stage in an opera at the end of Act I dressed in thick bear skin coats with a backdrop of blowing snow and Beigarth the Viking wearing a furry cap with horns has captured the beautiful Princess and with sword raised vows to make her love him, and we all sing "The cold makes us strong and brave! The winter winds strengthen our hearts and make us grateful for Beef Wellington with a light salad for we know proper diet is the secret of happiness. Hurrah!" Cue the curtain.

But as a Baptist I grow suspicious of spontaneous joy and tend to favor adversity with mild depression — that's just how I roll. Winter keeps me focused on decongestants and shoveling snow. When you're an old guy passing through heart attack country you pick up a snow shovel with trepidation, then you take a deep breath, and attack the driveway with the fatal heroism of Davy Crockett at the Alamo. Suddenly you feel closer to God. Really close.

Meanwhile the lazy non-leaf-rakers will see their yards ruined due to leaf rot and poisons in the soil. Their homes will decrease in value and the bank will foreclose and the families will move south to work in the sugar cane fields and their cars will sit on cinder blocks and their wives will be ravished by cruel land owners who wear suspenders over dirty undershirts. Those folks will wish a thousand times they had resisted autumn's drama and buckled down and raked their leaves like the good neighbors did.

Now, what was I talking about? Oh yea, Cancun and sea breezes.

Domesticated Caveman Fuzzy on the Details

You are relaxing with your cup of coffee and reading the headline in the newspaper, feeling glad that most of the problems in print belong to other people and not you. You begin to feel a little smug and safe and then your wife walks into the room and says, "Hon, notice anything different?"

She smiles.

This is a man's worse nightmare.

Awkwardness wraps around you like a hungry python. In an instant, she calls into play your ability to observe and to be cognizant of your surroundings which in this case is your wife. It forces a man, who has the attention span of a hummingbird, to stop and focus on something directly in front him and then he is expected to verbalize it all — and do it in an appropriate tone and manner. You suddenly realize the gates of Hell are yawning open just for you.

Your have just taken a direct hit, all engines are on fire — you need to land somewhere amidst the dense jungle. You grab your stomach, moan, and fake an onset of cramps with a touch of prostate cancer and a mild case of leprosy. You race upstairs to the bathroom remembering to groan, go inside, and lean with your back against the closed door. Your chest is heaving as though you've run a 10K marathon. You have to think fast!

This happened to me recently. It tests your skills.

You quickly go down a simple list of the obvious.

Was she naked? Any limbs amputated? Had her hair been highlighted with purples and reds? Was she bald? Had she gone Gothic with black clothes, silver chains — Oh God, was her nose pierced? Has she been in the hospital for the past two weeks and just returned home — you keep cards at the office just for this purpose. Had she been holding a butcher knife in both hands raised over her head? Clothes, oh please don't let it be clothes — I don't even know what *I'm* wearing half the time!

Then I remembered an article I read on an airplane trip written by a woman author. It was all about being honest. She wrote about how hiding the truth was not good, it caused stress and good relationships are founded on both parties being open and honest about all the issues of life. She said that honesty can diffuse many situations before they become a problem. Just be up front. Lead with the truth.

With newfound confidence I opened the door and slowly went downstairs acting as though all my health problems had been solved in just one sitting. I gazed at my wife but nothing different leaped out at me so, remembering what the lady author said, I looked her in the face and said,

"Nope Hon. I'm sure it's a good thing whatever it is but to tell the truth I really don't see anything different."

I smiled and shrugged, hoping it's that smile I had in college she told me was so irresistible. I looked her in the eyes with my eyes, my baby blues that she had fallen for years ago. I made no move to bolt from the room. I had now grabbed honesty by the horns.

Her eyes narrowed and she gave me a detailed account of the rigors of losing weight, having hair restyled, buying new smaller clothes (such as she was wearing now), and went on to explain the frustration of living with a blind caveman.

Though I told her later that the new dress and weight loss looked great and that maybe I have cataracts, there were nevertheless, consequences. I'm cooking a lot now and learning to make salads.

Domesticated Caveman Fuzzy on the Details

Guys, here is how you can avoid a string of strained and silent dinners.

First, act as though you are reading this column and ever so slowly pull a corner of the newspaper down towards you. Now moving only your eyes look at your wife sitting in the room with you and make some mental notes:

Count her arms and legs. Be sure to look carefully and count again.

Is she wearing an eye patch?

Is she holding a meat cleaver?

In the past week, has she been gone longer than a day?

Remember, thorough observation trumps honesty any day.

I'm a much smarter caveman now, I don't read on airplanes.

Doctor, I'm Tired of Pulling the Plow

Recently I went to my doctor for a check-up. This annual ceremony starts out with the doctor grasping my neck, to insure it is still there. Then I open my mouth and the good doctor makes sure I have all my teeth and only one throat.

The down part of the visit is when you're told to turn around, drop your pants, and you hear the snap of a plastic glove. There is movement behind you, you feel pressure — your eyes cross, your nostrils flare and you sing "Moon River" in soprano on your tippy toes. When the prodding is over you stare at the floor, humbled, while the doctor happily announces the prostate is firm — thrilled like he had just found a good cantaloupe.

I hoped this year would be different. My schedule has been hectic and I'm tired. I hoped my doctor would say I have severe exhaustion. I've always thought that was a sophisticated sounding ailment associated with famous people like Earnest Hemmingway, Liza Minnelli, and Elton John.

My problem was symptoms. I needed some. I Googled "severe exhaustion" and got nothing. I wondered about flaring nostrils (oops, that's the prostate) or continual sobbing noises that occur on Monday mornings just before work.

The heroes of the black and white movies had severe exhaustion all the time, and people carried them to luxurious beds, got them water, and opened the window. Sometimes Dracula flew in for a visit.

I wanted to go to one of those hospitals that have all young female nurses. You sit around all day by the pool in a white bathrobe and silk neck scarf while they bring you crab dip and imported water.

What I crave is relaxation per medical recommendation — slack time with no guilt.

But my doctor is a no nonsense Baptist, a local guy who was brought up on a farm and is a proponent of practicality. If my sinuses are clogged up he says to hose some salt water up both nostrils.

Memory loss? How would I know?

Heart pain? Sure, but instead of asking me about the crush I had on my high school homecoming queen and how that turned out, he brings in an EKG machine. They put me on a table, connect me to wires, and instruct me to be very still. They tell me I'm doing a great job while the machine hums, doors open and close, and hushed voices in the hallway pass by outside.

This longing for special health care goes back to my youth. I wanted sympathy and to be favored above my two sisters. I imagined lying on a bed gazing up at the ceiling as though I was fighting a horrible sickness. My mother would say, "Oh what a brave boy! We were wrong to have ever punished him for anything. We should get him a pony." In a small sickly whisper I would say "Thank you. God bless," and my head would fall back upon the pillow. In my fantasy my sisters would be sold to pay for the horse.

I wish my doctor would demand I do nothing for a year, but only very famous people get that and only if they've trashed a hotel room or fail to show up for their own concert.

They unplug me and pronounce me fit. I sit up, put on my shirt and prepare to go back to pulling the plow. My son needs to be moved to college, we're going to Ohio this summer, church activities are scheduled, there are columns to write, the boxer needs to be walked, garage cleaned out, and guests are coming to dinner.

I figure my first chance to collapse will be the fall.

Becoming a Cowboy — the Nu-Way

I ordered a new dog collar for our boxer and when it came it was too big — which made me glad. This would call for a trip to downtown to a shoe store called Nu-Way. They can cut the collar down to size, and besides, I love any excuse to go to that store.

Not only do they repair and sell shoes, but they sell cowboy boots and hats. You step through the door, old wood floorboards creak, and you smell leather and shoe polish. Next you hear the machines located in the back of the store, the clatter of sewing and stitching. People actually *work* there; they do things that call for skill and craftsmanship. The 1920s character of the place makes you feel you've stepped back in time but with modern merchandise. It's the boots and cowboy hats that get me — those and the huge stuffed Tom turkey at the door as you come in. Shoe cobblers with guns. Who'da thought?

I've always wanted a pair of boots and a hat from Nu-Way — to express my powerful masculinity. But my wife tells me over breakfast one morning, "You can't wear boots and a hat…you're too geeky."

That is a direct hit. My ego takes on water and slowly lists to starboard.

"Am not," I put my coffee cup down and look her in the eyes. "I've sired offspring, and I like rodeos."

Big Decisions Are Best Made with Hotdogs

"Sweetie," she says, sitting her coffee cup down, "the sight of you in boots and a hat would prevent any 'siring'— it would be a form of birth control — and you'd scare the horses!"

She cackles, picks up her coffee and reaches for the newspaper.

My ego sinks silently beneath the cold dark waters of shame.

I go to Nu-Way and while I wait for the collar to be cut I wistfully handle boots and hats that catch my eye. I pick up manly man boots like Noconas in deep rich colors with pointed toes. Some boots are polished and some are rustic. Some of the cowboy hats have a formal "Sunday go to meeting" cut and some are rough and bent to show strength and character — like me, deep down inside.

I try a hat on for fun and suddenly I'm walking down the streets of old Dodge City wearing new snakeskin boots, Wrangler jeans, a western shirt and a big Stetson hat on my head. I turn a corner and see a beautiful woman crying for help. She wears a blue gingham dress, has thick blond hair down to her shoulders, a pencil thin waist with white cowgirl boots. She is being pulled back and forth between two evil looking outlaws all dressed in black with dirty boots and sloppy old hats.

"Get your hands off her you mangy dogs!" I yell and step towards them.

All three look at me and stop.

"Eeuuuw!" says the woman staring at me wide eyed.

Both men release the woman, look at each other, then me and one says, "Who's the geek in the birth control boots and hat?" A nearby horse looks in my directions, shrieks like a woman, sits down, and covers both eyes with its front hooves.

The threesome all point at me and snicker. One of the men pulls his gun, aims at my feet and says "Dance!" and then —

"Mister? Can I help you?" I realize one of the Nu-Way clerks is talking to me.

"No," I say sadly, "you really can't but thanks." I put the hat back on the rack.

I pay for the collar and with my head hanging low I shuffle past the boots and hats and exit out the door.

Come spring I guess I'll get some Birkenstock sandals. Yippee. I. Aye.

The Diet of a Pharisee

The cardiologist finished the test, gave me a $250 per visit Look-Of-Concern and then advised me to lose some weight. I started living off of salads made from lichen, algae, small twigs, and grass clippings and skipped the Thousand Island dressing. But occasionally I awake from a deep stupor and find myself under a tree on my stomach with my forearms resting on the half eaten carcass of a deer, my face bloody and sticky. I bare my front teeth and lick my hands clean. Well yes — of course I'm disappointed with myself, but raw deer is pretty good when you are hungry and by the time you chase one down you're famished.

When I tell people I have to diet I wish they'd say things like "No way! You're fabulous, handsome and your stomach isn't sagging at all." Instead they give me a knowing smile and tell me about different diets they have tried. A friend told me about diet peanut butter and nodded her head as though I should have tried it already. Apparently people are seeing quite enough of me.

I've learned you can also lose weight by increasing your metabolism. I found where I can buy pills to increase my metabolic rate to that of an adolescent rabbit but the address is a P.O. box in Moosejaw, Alaska. They want cash in small denominations.

Big Decisions Are Best Made with Hotdogs

    I could join a male support group like Men Enthused Over Weight loss (MEOW) and sit with hefty size men drinking decaf coffee out of Styrofoam cups while they describe how as boys they were told to eat everything on their plate — because there were children in Africa that would love to eat broccoli. These men now feel they were tricked into being enormous. This dredges up issues and they realize they have been deceived by their mothers. Their big shoulders begin to shake and they start to cry and hug each other and realize now where their guilt issues have been coming from all their lives. They vow to pursue new interests like painting with watercolors and eating organic. Don't get me wrong, I have no problem with men crying and hugging just as long as I'm not involved. It makes me nervous and then I get a bad case of the munchies.

    The only way to lose weight is to accept a zero-tolerance policy while looking in the mirror and admit you can't wear plaids and polyester anymore. Smile and remember that great things can be done with plankton and arugula. Use your imagination regarding water.

    How will I tackle weight loss? Through conceit per the Bible, that's how. While you people eat your steak, creamed potatoes, and chocolate pie, I will sip my bone marrow consommé and look down my nose at you. I will think myself better than you due to my self-control. I will thank God that I am not as you are and glorify the Almighty in that He has lifted me up from the miry clay of indulgence and set my feet on bean curd and crowned me with light headedness.

    I will harness conceit and self-righteousness together like a team of horses and let them pull me up the hill of small boring meals. I will stand on street corners and glare as you pull up to fast-food drive-throughs and point my finger and judge you to be gluttons while I lick a stalk of celery. I intend to put the self-righteous Pharisee within me to work.

    But first, I think some deer and a milkshake would be nice.

The Day My Barber Left Town

When I was young and moody any change was good but when you get on the far end of fifty it seems nothing changes for the better nor does it completely heal and so you grieve for the first leaf that falls in autumn and wince when your tennis elbow flares up. So I went to my medical specialist — together we're putting his kids through college — pointed to my offending elbow and he injected my arm with steroids and I thanked him. No problemo.

Having mended my wing and contributed to higher education, I walked outside into a warm sunny day with clear blue skies, which naturally put me the mood for a haircut.

But my barber, Jim, had left town for two weeks. I rode around the city hoping, looking, and slowing down to peer at storefronts that might contain a barber. Finally, I found myself in a mall standing in front of a hair salon that said, "Professional Hairstylist. Walk-ins Welcome," so I walked in.

Everything was black and white. The floor was black tile and the chairs were black too. The walls were white with big mirrors and there were posters of men and women looking insulted and anemic dressed in black leather with rows of rings in their ears and their thumbs jammed into the front pockets of their jeans. A mobile was suspended from the ceiling made of objects like a tennis ball (black), a spoon (white) and a plastic pair of scissors (black). The magazines had themes about being "All Woman" — even the National Geographic's were about that.

A young lady appeared from out of nowhere wearing black leather and white earrings with black and white streaked hair — I realized she had been standing in front of me, camouflaged — and said her name was Star and asked me how I was doing. I said I was fine. She appeared to be eighteen, but at my age half the population looks eighteen.

"Dja know whatcha want?" she asked, chewing and popping some gum.

I wanted to say "my normal," but I didn't think Star was familiar with normal so I told her just a trim and I shrugged as though this wasn't a big deal. I'm Baptist, beauty is not what we're about — it's your soul that's important, that and stories about Hell and being humble.

"First time here?" (Pop!) she said. I replied yes, which completely satisfied her curiosity about me. She began to cut and snip. In ten minutes she removed the black and white zebra patterned smock, turned me to face the mirror and asked, "Howszat?" (Pop!)

I looked and saw an aging man whose hair was chopped and spiked — like I'd just sat down on a nail. But I was raised to always be polite so I told her it was fine, thank you very much, paid her, and left. If this was a trim then my rear end was a keyboard.

I walked through the mall, anticipating women swooning and having pamphlets thrust at me advertising intervention programs. I found an old NC State baseball cap in my truck and pulled it down tight on my head.

I got home angry and full of regrets about what I should have said, like the way most people get thirty minutes after something happens.

My wife was stirring a pot of spaghetti sauce when I walked in and when she saw me take off my cap she put the big spoon down and said, "Well, look at you."

"Yeah?" I growled.

"Yes, you've got the most beautiful blue eyes. Come here sailor."

7

The Animals in My Life

When It Snows I Carry a Mule

The Devil Wears Fur and Watches Desperate Housewives

Bureaucracy Got the Bull

Squirrel Threatens Nice Man Over Birdfeeder

Building a Nest Calls for Compromise

When It Snows I Carry a Mule

I survived the Great Christmas Snow Event of 2010 and learned a few things. Depending on your age the storm was either "awesome" or a "humdinger!" Of course some people will sniff and say it didn't compare with the great Halloween Thunderstorm of 1937, the April Tax Day Tornado of 1964, or the July 4th Volcano of 207 B. C.

Nevertheless for the South it was a proper storm. It came duly announced and with good manners. It didn't blow things around or disrupt power. It arrived on time, did what it was suppose to do, then moved on. Elected officials could learn a lot from such a storm.

The storm probably broke some records, and we know the only records that count are those that occurred during the Boomer generation. Storms that do not break records are just, well, weather. And we get a lot of that.

After a few weeks of seeing the white stuff turn black and dirty you move past the point where polite small talk can be made by referring to the storm. If today you were in the waiting room at the doctor's office passing time and said to someone next to you, "Boy, that snow was something wasn't it?" they would respond with a thin smile, shudder, and quietly move to another seat.

We don't prepare well for snowstorms here in the South — we'd rather plan a barbecue. When Snowcalypse hit I found myself at the grocery store with the other 26, 000 people in Statesville. I remember passing the bread section that was overrun by a teeming mob of frantic people. I observed one brave man who had picked up the last French baguette. He brandished the baguette at the oncoming mob like Davy Crockett swung his empty musket at the Mexican troops when they overran the Alamo. "It's mine!" the man shouted as the horde of bread crazed zombies came at him. I heard him scream as he went down, and I turned my head and moved on. I had just popped in for some barbecue sauce.

Such storms bring cold which in the South is anything less than 34 degrees, and Southerners are not used to that. We don't dress properly and when we go outside it burns through our skin. You stand on a street corner alone and feel like a Christian martyr that told Caesar you would not relinquish your faith so he gave you a choice to die by lions or freezing and you chose this. You realize now you may have made a mistake.

My father used to say that we don't get storms like we used to. He would tell us about the time he was caught in a blizzard while walking 200 miles to school. He was lucky enough to find a stray mule, killed it, gutted the carcass and crawled inside to keep warm. The storm lasted for days then it turned very cold. So he stayed there inside the mule and built a small kitchen with a gas stove, a nice living area, and read by candlelight. He crawled out in the spring and walked the rest of the way to school — barefoot.

We are better people for winter experiences. Now I've learned to keep emergency supplies like cans of Vienna sausages, Lance cheese crackers, and canned drinks in the backseat of the car. And with a nod to my father's story, I'm considering keeping a spare mule in the trunk.

The Devil Wears Fur and Watches Desperate Housewives

The Devil is in my house.

It's just before dawn and I'm writing this column using only the soft light of my computer monitor. I dare not use more illumination as it could draw attention. I've learned to listen for the soft click-click of paws on our hardwood floor. I've trained myself to look for eyes so brown they blend into the dark shadows of corners and hallways and can stare at you for hours. You sense your every move is being watched, evaluated, judged.

Oh, I miss the days when I was my own man! My freedom is dwindling away little by little, like a winter day blending into a cold dark night.

So how did my life take such a startling turn from a normal man who's only worries were clean underwear, finding his car keys every morning, and making sure he took the garbage out before Wednesday?

My young son wanted a dog.

Well, what kid doesn't? I grew up on a farm with dogs, cats, hogs, snakes, cattle, and the occasional hurt-sparrow-that-you-nurse-back-to-health. This request for a dog was, I thought, I good sign.

Big Decisions Are Best Made with Hotdogs

The kid was growing up. Enough with the Legos and Barney the Dinosaur.

We went over the ground rules. First, it was his dog, not mine. He'd have to take care of it, which meant feeding and watering it each day, and he'd have to play with it. That was important. A dog is an intelligent creature, they are not things. They have feelings, they understand basic things like kindness, and can be taught good things as well as bad things. My son agreed to everything.

The family met, which is to say we had a large meat lover pizza delivered to the house and discussed the issue around our kitchen table. Details were hammered out. I thought we had an agreement.

A vet friend of mine called one day and let me know there was a litter of full-blooded boxer puppies at his office. Come take my pick and bring the checkbook.

And so evil entered my house in the form of a puppy. She was a full blood Fawn Boxer. Her little paws were white with fawn brown fur on her upper body. Her chest was snow white and she had black around the eyes and the cutest upturned little muzzle. We named her Roxey, and we were all struck by her beauty. But then sin and evil are a delight to the eye, the Bible says so.

At first my son played with her and fed her. Those were good days. Roxey would roll around in the floor and you could tickle her fat little stomach. She liked that. My son talked to her, took her into his room. I read the newspaper and controlled the remote. Life was good.

Then one day my son turned a bit sulky, he learned to play soccer, then softball, and he learned to ride a bicycle. Then there was a girl and all too soon it seemed, it fell to Dad to make sure the dog was walked and fed and played with. Dad cleaned up the poop, and Dad paid the vet bills. Coming home after work meant taking care of Roxey — first thing. I had a dog.

Months and months went by then one day the boxer chewed the bottom off our sofa and I went ballistic! My wife picked the puppy up over her shoulder and hugged her.

"It's alright my sweetie pie," crooned my wife. " My good girl, yes you are — you're just a sweet good girl!"

Turning to me she said sternly, "You should walk her more. If you did, then this would not happen. You should be more sensitive to the needs of others. I've always thought you were self-centered. Your mother always suspected you were bipolar."

As my wife carried "good girl" out of the room, the boxer looked over my wife's shoulder. Her eyes fixed on me and in my mind I heard, "Watch what I do to your shoes — the new pair, those Cole Palmers that you love so much." I swear I thought I felt the room grew cold — I could see my breath.

The boxer grew bigger and could do no wrong.

One afternoon Roxey managed to eat a cake that was left on the countertop. My wife thought it was hilarious. She never thought it was hilarious when I did it.

As she knelt down to hug Roxey, the dog looked over my wife's shoulder at me and for an instant I thought the boxer leered at me with black and green teeth and then her head twisted completely around while staring at me! It seemed that the kitchen window was covered with black flies, but when I started to speak everything went back to normal. My wife turned to me and said, "You can run out and get a cake (she looks me up and down), if you think you really *need* a dessert." She looked at my stomach like it was something you'd step on by accident.

The boxer trotted out of the room behind my wife, but not after looking back at me and grinning with those green rotten teeth and her eyes momentarily turned red with slits, like a demon.

The boxer now claims what was my chair, naps on what was my footrest, and watches *Desperate Housewives* from my couch. If I try to correct any of this I am met with cold stares by my wife, my son, and the dog. They have become the unholy Trinity.

Each day now I come home but it's not *my* home. I have my list of chores, and I know I must do them before I can eat. There is fresh food to be put in the dog's dish, fresh water to be drawn from the faucet, and any scattered rubber toys are to be picked up and placed next to Roxey's dog couch. The couch is from LL Bean and her water and food bowls were handmade by a potter in New York. I'm making payments.

Roxey likes a five-minute brush down and then it's outside to run around the back yard. I run, the dog watches.

Roxey has been observing me a lot lately. She demands longer walks; more play time and more treats.

Oh. My. Goodness. I see that she is in the room with me right now. She slipped in quietly, unnoticed and she knows that I am writing about her. She stares at me, silently, intently. She steps closer to me and gives me a commanding stare.

The Devil is now waiting to be walked — and she likes to be scratched behind her ears.

Bureaucracy Got the Bull

I have a great job but like many good jobs, it comes with stress. Surprises are usually not welcomed but there are exceptions.

My office, part of a city owned utility complex, is located on a rural highway called Bell Farm Road. The office site is surrounded by beautiful dairy farms and sits on about 260 acres of rolling pasture land enclosed behind a steel fence.

One sunny weekend I was going in to the office to catch up on some paper work and was surprised to see standing beside our automatic steel entrance gate, an enormous reddish colored bull — pawing the ground. He was a complete unmodified male full of testosterone and capable of attitude changes at the drop of a hat. He looked lost and in need of directions.

He was the type you see at rodeos, a big boy Brahma, later estimated at around 1600 pounds of beef, who was used to doing things his way and could throw a problem or a man off his back at will. He dwarfed several of our pick-up trucks. I asked around but no one knew who owned him and no one on our staff wanted to see if he was carrying a business card. City policy is to turn away visitors who do not have appointments however this bull, I later named him Big Mac, ignored our rule with impunity and followed me through the gate. No, I wasn't going to get out and stop him.

He wandered over to a huge tree and began to eat grass while standing in the shade. He definitely had some smarts.

I grew to like Big Mac. As the days passed, he showed up with the rest of us at 8 a.m. and he clocked out around 5 p.m. going back into the woods located on our site to maybe toss back a few drinks and hang out with the squirrels. He ate grass in areas we could not maintain, which was a good thing, and he would nod to everyone that passed by as though he was wishing them to have a great day. He was a good bull, listened without interrupting and kept the grass trimmed around our fences better than ever before.

Big Mac never complained, did not start gossip, reported to work prepared, showed initiative and he specialized in grounds maintenance. No one stepped forward to claim him and upon reflection, I guess that could have given him some self esteem problems. I suspected he probably had some confinement issues from his past to deal with, too.

Big Mac did not share any of that with me mind you — I just put two and two together. Sometimes he looked at me as if he wanted to tell me something then appeared to change his mind and resumed eating more grass. He just wanted to be there where things were quiet and where he was needed. The old bull had found what we all seek — peace and enjoyment in his work. He asked for nothing but his space.

I reported Big Mac's presence to the proper divisions of our organization and I saw their eyes narrow in bureaucratic apprehension. They saw liability risks with 1600 pounds of bull running loose. Still worse, Mac had not filled out an employment application and probably had no valid North Carolina driver's license — a big must in our organization. We're funny about procedure and numbers and Mac simply did not fit into the system. The wheels of government turned and Big Mac's days began drawing to a close.

I knew I was going to miss the old bovine and those eyes of his that seemed to understand life and how it was to be enjoyed — under shade trees with plenty of fresh air. I would walk the grounds in the afternoon and would find Mac chewing grass. I'd tell him about the day, about people, about who was sick, about dumb things that happened. Big Mac took it all in.

I began to tell him about my fears, how things are changing, and wondered if he felt it in his bones like I did. Life sort of shuffles you around some times, and I wondered if Mac was fearful of the future.

I once told Mac about a friend of mine, recently diagnosed with cancer, his future wasn't very bright. Mac stopped chewing for a moment, seemed to consider what this meant, as though this was something that demanded concern on his part. Mac was like that, a respectful bull.

Then one day I told him that government policy and officials, after all these weeks, had reached a decision and that he couldn't stay. Didn't matter that he'd done a great job with the grass and trim work. People were coming for him.

Late one afternoon a big truck designed to move livestock, pulled up at our gate. Some men got out — they had ropes.

The grass is growing back in those hard to reach places and you don't have to be too careful where you step now. I try to remember what Mac showed me so that when Divine policy ends my time I will have found peace, have done good work, and will be missed. We should all be so lucky.

Squirrel Threatens Nice Man Over Birdfeeder

I like birds.

I like to watch bright red Cardinals, territorial Blue Jays, yellow Finches, grey and black Chickadees, and orange-breasted Robins. I especially like to see them gather around my new bird feeder.

Anyone can see that my bird feeder is strictly for birds — it even has some writing on the bottom that says "Bird Feeder, Model #67309." I keep it full of birdseed.

However a local squirrel has decided that this is his own personal squirrel feeder. He's pushy, possessive, a real jerk squirrel. I think he's from up North.

I say "his" because this is definitely a guy squirrel.

If it was female, the squirrel would have convinced me that I *wanted* her to eat out of the feeder and that I had been selfish and shallow as long as she has known me. Having planted the seed of guilt, she then she would have had me move the feeder around the yard to see how it looks in a corner or close to the deck or beside a red maple. I would have complied.

But the big give-away that this particular squirrel is a guy is found in the fact that he does not put the feeder lid back down when he's through — definitely a male squirrel.

I decided to scare this guy squirrel so bad that he'd never come back. I went upstairs into my son's room and rummaged through his closet, past DVDs, old baseball caps, socks, lost underwear, etc. until I found his Daisy BB air rifle. I smiled.

A chilly Saturday morning found me sitting under a bush in the back yard. The bush concealed me and gave me a perfect shot at ol' Fur Face. I got in place and turned my ball cap around until the brim was backwards on my head. I was cold and kept my hands in my pockets. I needed to keep my resolve; I softly hummed "Onward Christian Soldiers."

Suddenly there he was! He emerged out of the woods, jumped from a nearby fence, landed on the feeder and raised the lid. I decided to go for a rear end shot and lined him up in my sights. I had pumped the gun four extra times to make sure the BB would have some sting in it. I took aim, right where he had no hair, eased back on the trigger and fired.

A direct hit! I even heard it "SMACK!" when it hit his butt. The squirrel jumped about three feet in the air and ran up the nearest tree in a long blurred gray line, like you see in cartoons. I managed to get off another shot but missed. He ran to the top of the tree, sat on a limb, looked down and began scolding me in that rasping "chukka, chukka" sound made by angry or embarrassed squirrels.

An hour later he had the nerve to try again. This time I was able to sneak up close to him using a line of bushes for cover. I was less than five feet from him when I took aim, at the same bare spot I had hit earlier ,and pulled the trigger. The squirrel screamed the equivalent of "Holy Crap!" and ran across the yard leaving a trail of little brown squirrel nuggets behind him. He ran up a tree, sat on a branch and cried about the woes of life, the fickleness of nature, the plight of the polar bear, and the condition of impoverished people everywhere. Oddly, he sounded Sicilian.

I just shook my trusty Daisy back at him and laughed— two males trying to communicate.

Squirrel Threatens Nice Man Over Birdfeeder

Later that day I was sitting on my deck feeling very in control of life when with a start I realized the squirrel was on a corner of my roof. Apparently he had been staring down at me for some time. It was a cold disdainful stare.

I sat up and stared back into his dark black eyes. His silent intense stare conveyed a message to me, a subtle threat, played on my nerves.

"Soon," he seemed to imply," you sleep with the fishes." He bobbed his head as if for emphasis then he scampered off.

His manner, so confident and with purpose, set me to thinking. Not that it bothered me too much, mind you, but I have considered installing an alarm system in the house. And does anyone know if you can get a remote to start a car?

Building a Nest Calls for Compromise

I'm watching a pair of robins outside my window. They are in a dogwood tree and appear to be building a nest.

The Missus is busy arranging twigs and straw in just the right way. Sometimes she's not pleased so she rearranges a stick by putting it in another part of the nest. Mr. Robin is watching at a distance.

The old fellow has been trying to help out. He drags in things he finds — old pieces of straw, a badly bent twig, a faded piece of ribbon — stuff that he finds lying around. For him it's just a big bother. The wife tosses out half of everything he brings in — it's junk. He never was one for decor and organization. She has always been the one to build the nest, and he is trying to stay out of her way right now. They both seem a bit agitated.

He has a worried look on his face as most expectant fathers do. He turns his head from side to side looking at her, gauging her mood, and then looks out at my yard. It rained recently and you'd expect the worms to come up for air and bugs to fly looking for a dry place. But I keep the yard sprayed and cover is sparse so there is not as much food there as one might think.

Obviously, he chose the wrong yard — again.

She wanted to spend the summer in the country where the soil is rich, and there is a much better selection of bugs and worms. But no, Mr. I-Know-Everything wanted to be in the city. He thought they would save a lot of energy by working a small yard and that would give him plenty of time for things he wanted to do. Did he think so much about what she wanted to do? No he did not.

She is also worried about the kids. Growing up in a city full of cats, pesticides, bi-polar squirrels, and people that trim trees is not so safe, she thinks. The smell of charcoal grills aggravates her allergies. They could do better and she means to put her foot down next year.

He has always been headstrong. Sometimes she tries to remember what she saw in him back in the early days when it was all about flying in big flocks and staying up way past sundown. They use to catch big juicy bugs that came out late in the evening and sometimes they could get a caterpillar or two. They were young then and they loved to bath together in the park and preen their feathers in the sun. They flew for hours just enjoying each other's company. Now give him a moth and five minutes later he farts, scratches, and takes a nap.

The past winter was brutal. They spent most of it trying to find shelter. Once during a really bad snowstorm they were sitting on a branch in a big oak tree. She was about to freeze when he put his wing over her to shield her from the wind and sleet. While they huddled there she looked up and saw that some of his facial feathers were beginning to turn gray. The cold bothers them more each year.

And now they are here. She was about to throw out a bit of cloth he had offered when she thought better of it. As he watches, she puts his contribution in a nice place and his big red breast swells with pride. He sits up a bit taller. She shakes her head and tidies up the nest as her sweet old fool flies off, believing he is in complete control.

8

The Sweet & Funny of Life

A Quick Glimpse Over the Edge

A New Laptop Computer Brings Me in Line

Men Should Do as They Are Told, It's Cheaper

Man Ponders Mortality Under a Car

I'll Take Two Hamburgers without the Palm Trees

I Got the Sears Closed-Up-and-Shutdown-Blues

I Don't KitchenAid Anymore

Kisses Sweeter Than — Mustard

Hard Work Teaches You a Song and the Way Home

Free Therapy and Inner Peace, Right Here!

For All the Waiting People of the World
The Class of 1971 Has My Heart — and My Stomach
Blue Skies and Each Individual Leaf Is a Wonder
The Taming of a Man
We Need to Bake More Cakes
Soap or Consequences
Sir, Your Screams Are Forgiven
Sex in the Secret Service Reminds Me of Superman
Please Tell Me Where Is Up?
No, I'm Not William H. Macy
Mommies Make the Best Dancers

A Quick Glimpse Over the Edge

My ancestors were very religious people and as soon as they stepped off the boat they shot the Indians, set up a budget, formed a committee, and built a church. They proclaimed themselves Baptists, were suspicious of pleasure (it usually brought on trouble), condemned dancing, and believed the presence of God was strongest in the back three pews.

But as time passed they felt even this was simply not enough restrictions and so in the late 1940s they pulled away from the Southern Baptist Convention and became known as Original Free Will Baptists. Most were farmers so I grew up in a church where the men had white foreheads, our Broadman Hymnal was green, oscillating fans kept the heat bearable in the summer, and you were expected to pay attention during the sermon. Attention Deficit Disorder was cured by your parents or any other adult who told you to sit still, be quiet and listen. If a warning didn't work you got smacked — and that always worked. We were not pill people.

I grew up inhaling second hand smoke and standing upright in the car seat as my father drove down country roads at 70 mph in a 1959 Ford. Johnny Horton sang about the "Battle of New Orleans," ground beef was our friend, and butter made everything taste better. Kids these days are raised using ten-foot shelves of books accompanied by excuses. I was raised by pure chance and love.

Lately I've been thinking about those times and I miss the joy. We were wonderfully naive back then. A cigarette was your link to Hollywood movies and you guffawed at corny jokes. We thrived on ignorance and everybody thought Lassie was just one dog.

Now we have too much information, too many guardrails, too much black and yellow tape, and warnings "Do not touch, glowing charcoal may be hot," "Sharp, razor may cut skin if pressed into it," "Open with extreme misgivings — see Therapist." It takes a wrench and a knack for riddles to open your pill bottle. Everything is potentially harmful to you.

I'm tired of the stress so last week, on pure impulse, I drove all the way to work with my seat belt unfastened. Yep. I did — NahNahNahNahNah, Naah! It was a cheap thrill. The Angel of Death rode shotgun and I felt young and reckless again. You're the first person I've ever told about this.

Death, we all have to face it with or without a seatbelt.

One day the doctor will stride into the room holding a report and with dark concern on his handsome, Botoxed photogenic face say, "Your jangular expialadocious is disseminated. You have two months to live. I can make you comfortable but that's it. Also, I'm out of town all next month."

"No problem. I'll handle it," I say. I shop the nearest grocery store for ten cartons of unfiltered Camel cigarettes. The cashier is horrified and swoons to the floor. I walk out holding the cigarettes and six cases of Land O' Lakes butter under my arm. I rip one stick out of the box, peel the wax paper down like a banana peel, and eat it while strolling down the street. People try to intervene or give me pamphlets. "Stuff it," I say and walk home and I light up a Camel and my nervous system rings like a submarine preparing to submerge.

I make gallons of Nestlé's chocolate milk with too much chocolate (Hi, Mom!), put on a Mel Tormé CD and soon word gets out. Neighbors, who for years have been slaves to their kid's safety obsessed, bipolar needs, find their way to my house. I grill steaks every day, we jump in the pool with our clothes on — we all stop eating vegetables.

Every now and then it's good to break free. No, I haven't gone over the edge yet, but I am peeking at it. Join me.

A New Laptop Computer Brings Me in Line

With one purchase and submission of my ID and password, I have logged into the modern world. I recently bought a laptop computer. I'm high on a feeling of accomplishment. Even my seventeen year old believes dad pulled one out of the hat this time. He handed me the highest compliment a kid can give a parent these days, he said, "Awesome!" Be still my heart.

The laptop has a built in camera, a first class sound system with special er, uh, stuff that allows me to listen to radio stations and play CDs for music and even handles DVDs for movies. With the built in camera and video capabilities (webcam) I can look at people in real time while they look at me. My mother used to call that "staring" and said it was rude.

The laptop can probably open the garage door and comb my hair but I have not figured that out yet. There are no messy cables for a printer or the Internet because (drum roll please) it is wireless! I'm always connected to the world. My little "snookums" (it's just so cute) is about the size of a notebook and fits into a black case with a shoulder strap that projects a very European look as I stroll through the Food Lion parking lot.

Big Decisions Are Best Made with Hotdogs

Oh yeah, it will do computer stuff too.

Columbus sailed to the new world without email, laptop, or an Internet connection relying solely on his wits, hard tack biscuits, and good eyesight. But now I can prop my laptop on a nearby grocery cart and quiz Google on the finer points of spotting a good cantaloupe in the produce department. I use to think myself better than people with laptops hanging from their shoulders and now I am one.

We are obsessed with the Internet and keeping enormous amounts of data at our fingertips. There was a time when being an engineer, a textile worker or a machinist was a long-term profession, but those people were let go and our ability to manufacture things (my lap top was made in China) was given away by liberals — traitorous behavior later embraced by Texas conservatives and continued by the new administration of Blame and Arrogance.

We now spew out words by the gazillion. My column demands I be a wordsmith and I pass out-of-work engineers and carpenters on my way to the newspaper office so I can add to the already trillions of words out there in the world. When the Chinese versions of "Tiny" and "Muscles" come to collect our national debt they will find people that cannot make a light bulb but have fantastic communication devices and boatloads of data. We are a nation of electronic bytes — not industrial steel.

Some days ago my thoughts turned dark about the future, and I thought it would be nice to hurl myself in front of an oncoming bus, but I had a 10 a.m. dental appointment and you know how those people are if you are a no show. Later I did a live chat with a good friend that was online. I lamented the loss of carburetors, Roy Rogers' plastic boot drinking cups, hoboes, good manners, neighborhood newsstands, and drugstore chocolate sundaes. By the time I was through chatting I felt better, took a deep breath, and went to the refrigerator for a snack.

I am now ready to fall in line like baby ducks that follow their mother down to the pond, one little duckling after the other with me bringing up the rear — a laptop hanging from my shoulder. Awesome.

Men Should Do as They Are Told, It's Cheaper

All my wife wanted me to do was push the "Start" button at a specific time so our oven would bake a roast she had placed in it. She would be bringing four of her friends over for dinner that evening and the roast had to be ready. I mumbled something like, "Sure no problem."

However there *was* a problem. It was Saturday and I was trying to write this column. I had a serious case of word blockage with a pending deadline. My mind was blank, it refused to think, and all I could hear was a clock ticking away towards the deadline. I needed words or thoughts or maybe shock therapy.

I tried everything to get the words to flow. I drank orange juice, ate a prune, took multi-vitamins, swallowed something that contained Omega 3, finished an old prescription for acne, rearranged things on my desk, opened a box of dog biscuits (I've always wondered how they taste…like cardboard), stacked ten pencils on top of each other in a square, drank three cups of coffee, stared out the window, and was considering sniffing some paint thinner when a sudden stab of creativity hit and I hurried to the keyboard.

Big Decisions Are Best Made with Hotdogs

It all happened in a rush — projectile wordage. With the force of a fire hose, the words poured out the tips of my fingers and onto the keyboard. Phrases flowed like water down a mountain stream; wonderful adjectives came from out of nowhere. The approach to content and the syntax were nothing short of perfection. This was Hemmingway, Fitzgerald, Melville, Twain, and my ninth grade English teacher all rolled into one! I imagined my editor demanding I write a book based on this — he would cover the upfront costs with his kids' college fund.

Then I heard it, the sound of a car pulling up to our garage and I looked at the time. It was hours past the specified time that I was to have turned on the oven. There were five people outside of my house at this moment expecting to eat a roast that had not even started cooking. I heard car doors slamming.

I thought that if I could get to the oven and turn it on before my wife came in I could blame oven malfunction for the loss of dinner ("*See, I* did *turn it on, bad oven! Naughty oven! Gee Hon, hot dogs sound good to me!*"). But first I needed to save my masterpiece and in my haste I mistakenly clicked "NO" to the request to "SAVE." Hours of work were lost — I shrieked like I was at the dentist.

Then I remembered the oven. With my writing career now in shambles, I raced out of the den towards the kitchen. I figured I could hurl myself in front of a passing bus later that afternoon but right now I'd best attend to this pending dining disaster.

Then I discovered that our eighty-pound boxer had decided to lie around the corner of a doorway. I hit Roxey, the family's significant canine, at about sixty miles an hour. She was lying there like a big brown speed bump, and I was immediately airborne. My arms were stretched outward, and I remember marveling at how easy it is to fly; there was so little air resistance.

I belly landed, slid past the oven and the refrigerator, slowed to a stop, and was scrambling to my feet as the door opened to reveal my wife with her friends behind her. They all looked down at me and grimaced like I was something that needed to be cleaned up, now.

My wife never asked why I was half crouched panting or why the dog was barking and limping or who was the girl shrieking before she came in. She just said, "You didn't push the button did you?"

Men Should Do as They Are Told, It's Cheaper

FYI. Most restaurants can accommodate last minute seating for parties of five. All *you* need to do is send them your credit card, which is no problem. Your wife will take it for you.

Man Ponders Mortality Under a Car

I stepped out of my car. Lord knows I've done it a thousand times since I became a licensed driver. But this time was different.

I wasn't thinking much about traction and balance. The morning temperature was well below freezing and I forgot about black ice. If you had been watching me you would have thought some hidden monster grabbed my ankles, yanked, then pulled me underneath my vehicle.

They say it's not the destination but the journey that makes a trip. If that is true then I had an exciting time. There was the awareness that I was airborne looking up at blue skies and white clouds with my arms swinging in wide circles. My body was weightless and I anticipated bad things upon landing.

Funny what crosses your mind at times like that. Say, for instance, Mr. Allendale, my high school physics teacher. I realized the old codger had been right all along — there is gravity and there is mass and the two are eager to connect. I said ...a word... then hit the ground.

Finally, all was still, quiet. I had stopped and I opened my eyes.

I had never been underneath my car until that morning. Small metal pipes, long pieces of steel rods here and there at odd angles, and an oil pan were all inches above my face. I stared, dazed, at tubing, the backside of my tires, and at nuts and bolts screwed into the sides of things for seemingly no reason. Everything was colored muddy brown and smelled of earth and oil and seemed to say, "You don't belong here and you know it."

But there is something about landing after a fall that requires you take a moment and reflect. You want to establish that you are all right so you take inventory of joints and bones — count the stars in your eyes and if everything is all right you tingle with thankfulness. I wanted to get up quickly as though this never happened.

But if you ever find yourself down like that and alone — and if you have the time, I suggest you use some restraint and stay there a bit. All at once the fact that you are not paralyzed and will not need metal rods pushed into your spine to keep you upright or need other people to feed you sustenance through a straw brings a smile to your face. It is an "aha!" moment — you realize your days are numbered and full of trouble, you are small potatoes in a big world, that life is fleeting and fragile, and that for once you're glad that extra ten pounds went to your butt. There is a sudden enlightenment that comes with cheating the Grim Reaper.

From now on you intend to enjoy each day you are given and to stop being such a grouch. You wonder just how close the earth really has come to being hit by a huge asteroid but nobody knew about it and so you fell in love and bought the house and raised the kids and took that trip to the Grand Canyon all the while not knowing just how lucky you were. But now you know. Enlightenment.

So you make a mental note to help out more around the house and to call your mother tonight —"'cause, I love you mama." Appreciation, remorse, and redemption all in one day, enough to make a Baptist evangelist weep. God met Moses on the mountain to give him that information; me, He threw under a car.

Oddly enough the down side was — not enough injury. I was hoping for some good deep dark bruises to get me out of work, maybe even some sympathy but no such luck. A few scrapes and a light yellow bruise on my jaw was all I had to work with. The best I could muster was three days of stiffness and moans whenever I got up out of my recliner. But then, that is sort of normal for me, the stiffness and the groans, so no one noticed.

I'll Take Two Hamburgers without the Palm Trees

Somewhere at a posh resort a man in dark sunglasses and a white bathrobe sat under green palm trees considering his wealth while young nubile women brought him caviar and drinks with tiny umbrellas in them. But that man wasn't me.

I'd been running errands all afternoon and I had to hurry home and fire up the grill in order to have hamburgers done by the time expected guests arrived but I still needed to go by the cleaners, go by Lowe's, find an ATM, and stop by the post office. What I really needed was an outboard motor strapped to my back.

I try to avoid days like that but it's like trying to avoid a seasonal cold — you'll catch one every now and then despite good planning and excellent hygiene.

I'm checking things off my list when I remember we did not have any chocolate chip cookies — I consider them vegetables. I ducked into a store to get them and raced back out to the car, tossed the cookies in the seat beside me, threw the car in gear, and proceeded to race out of the parking lot. I had almost achieved orbital speed when I realized the cars I thought were leaving the parking lot were not moving at all — however I was.

Big Decisions Are Best Made with Hotdogs

I stood on the brakes with both feet and my car stopped but not before just touching the car ahead of me. The driver opened his door and got out.

He was an elderly gentleman with thin white hair and a cane. Despite the 90-degree heat he wore a thin navy blue cardigan sweater over a white knit shirt and khaki pants with new white sneakers. His shoulders were a bit drooped and he walked slowly towards me supported by his cane. I saw a lawsuit shuffling my way.

But instead of demanding to see my insurance card or dramatically feigning back pain he asked if I was all right. I said yes I was, introduced myself, apologized for the bump, and we shook hands. His hand was cold and trembled a bit with early Parkinson's. I asked if he was all right.

"Lord yes and that's saying a lot when you're eighty three!" he chuckled. Then he said, "Let's have a look-see at what we have here."

We inspected the bumpers, taillights, the muffler — looking for dings of any sort but could find nothing wrong on either car. We talked a bit more to see if either of us had mutual acquaintances in his city or mine but we did not.

"Well," he said, "lucky it's nothing. Have a nice day." He turned to walk away, stopped, looked back and said, "You take care, young fella."

I was amazed. In our litigious society simple forgiveness has almost gone the way of penny loafers and Studebakers. The old man had judged me with kindness; I was forgiven and free to go.

I pulled back into traffic shaking my head at what had just happened and then realized it had been a long time since I had been called "young fella." What a nice thing to say to me. My son thinks I'm so old you could put me in a glass case at the museum and schoolchildren could push a button and ask me questions about woolly mammoths.

I made it home and fired up the grill. I usually eat only one hamburger but I realized that a "young fella" can have two — with cheese. Both of mine were delicious!

What a day — youth and forgiveness with medium rare beef. That man under the palm trees has nothing on me.

I'll Take Two Hamburgers without the Palm Trees

I Got the Sears Closed-Up-and-Shutdown-Blues

It's spring and life is cheerful though one must accept certain grim realities like mortality, paper cuts, and the demise of our local Sears store. I will miss our Sears which had come to be like a friend to me that brought back memories of the old Sears & Roebuck store I knew when I was a boy.

That store had creaky wooden floors and was filled with toys, sporting goods, sewing machines, and appliances. The sales clerks were middle class working people who knew my parents by name and everyone agreed that Eisenhower should nuke Russia into a flat piece of glass. It was there my father purchased my first bicycle, and the clerk took me out back and helped me learn to stay upright on a moving two-wheeled object. You don't get that type of instruction on the Internet.

Imagine America in the 1880s. There were only thirty-eight states and about 65 percent of the people lived in rural areas. Only a dozen or so cities had 200,000 or more residents. One day a Chicago jewelry company accidently shipped some watches to a jeweler in a Minnesota hamlet who did not want them.

Richard Sears was an agent of the Minneapolis and St. Louis railway at a station in North Redwood, Minnesota. When he received a shipment of watches — unwanted by the Redwood Falls jeweler — Sears purchased them himself, sold the watches at a profit and ordered more for resale. In 1886, Sears began the R.W. Sears Watch Company in Minneapolis which expanded into other merchandise and became one of the first mail order houses in America supplying catalogues that contained about the only view of the world many people ever saw outside their own community. Old catalogues were carried to the outhouse where torn pages crinkled and used just right became the foundation of American hygiene.

As a child I lived for the Sears & Roebuck Christmas catalogues. The catalogue's arrival announced the holiday season and my mother would place the new catalogue on my bed so I would see it first thing when I came home from school. You were allowed to choose three items from it for Christmas but one item had to be clothing. Bummer. I would lie across the bed propped on my elbows and slowly turn each page and marvel at the new wonders of the year. The book was a holy document and each picture was a prophecy of the coming of Santa Claus. Today's Internet pictures have no holiness or wonder. They're just pixels. And you can't use them for hygiene.

The Sears company was founded by a romantic who dreamed of quality goods and service but in the early 1980s it fell into the hands of rapacious bandits that tore its heart out, refused to update the stores, streamlined the name to "Sears," and treated employees like outhouse catalogues.

And so I mourn the loss of my childhood and with it the loss of an icon of the American economy. Sears closing makes me sad, and I want to grab an old beat up guitar, sit on the front porch while wearing dark sunglasses, strum some old blues chords and sing:

"I wanted to buy some things today.

So I went down to Sears with my pay.

But the door was locked, a sign was in my way. I heard it on the evening news.

She's now lost to me and to you.

And that's why I got these Sears closed-up-and-shutdown blues."

Kisses Sweeter Than — Mustard

She was a big legged gal standing there with her arms wide open, water dripping off her long hair, and her lips pursed for a kiss. She leaned closer and began to wrap her arms around my neck. I love it when a woman takes the initiative.

She looked me in the eyes and planted a big kiss on me that started at the edge of my mouth and in her haste, slipped to my right cheek. Her bathing suit rubbed against my bare chest and I wrapped my arms around her and put my mouth to her ear and whispered, "I love you."

Then her mother took her hand and announced that it was naptime.

My two-year-old granddaughter and our family had been swimming at a cookout, and I was standing waist deep in the pool while she stood on the edge out of the water. It was time to go home and her mother had told her to give "Papa Joe" a goodbye kiss.

She held her mother's hand, turned and walked away — the chunky legs of a two year old moving quickly to keep up with an adult's stride. My lips now tasted of potato chips and hotdog with loads of mustard. A man doesn't forget a kiss like that.

I pushed away from the edge and did a slow backstroke thinking of all the kisses that define our lives.

The worse kisses start early in life. Aunt Grace, the old partially mummified spinster, sees you at a family gathering when you are about five years of age. She tells you that you are such a sweet boy she could just "eat you up" and moves towards you like a hungry predator. The liver spotted hands with fire-engine red fingernails reach out and hold your head in a cold firm grasp as her face moves down towards you. Lips, glossy red, move towards your forehead or cheek. You squirm. Like an incoming asteroid she quickly fills your field of vision and facial wrinkles begin to look like canyons coated with white powder. Her perfume is overpowering.

You pray that Jesus will call you up to heaven right then but Jesus sits still and never makes a sound — this is a test of endurance, not faith, kiddo. This near-death experience teaches men to seek women close to their own age and awakens theological ponderings as to what it takes for God to move on the plea " Help. Me."

But then things get better as the first romantic kiss comes into our lives. You're fourteen and at a community dance. She walked outside with you for some fresh air and there you are. The stage is set for a kiss.

But it's an awkward thing as we figure out what to do with our noses…do we lean our heads left or right to avoid a proboscis collision? But you figure it out and your lips go merrily about exploring this new world of warmth and delight. This ignites a determination in men to find a mate, and we begin to shake our antlers, paw the ground, and we buy cologne.

There are other kisses we get throughout life — the light kiss of a mother, the gentle peck of a sister, and then there is the special kiss that nudges you over the edge into love and a thirty-year mortgage.

But few kisses can compare to my chunky legged gal staging an exit. She knows how to lay one on you, hug your neck, and leave you with a memory as sharp as mustard.

Such sweet kisses — C'est l'amour!

Hard Work Teaches You a Song and the Way Home

Recently I was coming out of Asheville, NC on Interstate 40 and negotiating a very sharp curve while driving down a very steep mountain. I gripped the steering wheel and tried to keep the car from going off the road and into Forever. These are moments, as you wonder how far the car will actually fall if you miss the curve, that call for absolute concentration and bowel control.

The radio station I was listening to faded out and a local station came on. They announced "...old song by Tennessee Ernie Ford — 'Sixteen Tons'" — and there was Mr. Ford sounding just like I remembered him. That song always makes me think of muscular men with their sleeves rolled up swinging pick axes and hammers as they worked hard to earn their pay.

I identify with hard working people. When I was very young and during the summer months my father would come into my room about 5:30 in the morning while I was sound asleep. He would flip the light switch and harsh light would replace the darkness. Then he would say "Wake up. Let's go!" I would roll out of bed wondering why my sisters did not have to get up and feed the hogs. So young, yet I was already grappling with feminine equality.

Big Decisions Are Best Made with Hotdogs

I would find my "old clothes" — jeans with the knees worn out, a ragged short sleeve plaid shirt, any socks I saw on the floor, and my high top sneakers. I'd pull it all on and walk twenty-two steps down the hall to the kitchen where my mother would have cooked a breakfast of eggs, milk, and coffee — the air would be heavy with the smell of fried bacon.

We tried to wake up at the table with grunts that became monosyllables, which morphed into words until finally we spoke in complete sentences. At that point my father would give me the plan for the day. Then we would climb into his old green and white Ford truck we called "Big Green." The paint was missing in places, both bumpers were bent at odd angles and the cab was littered with glass Pepsi bottles. Small Moleskine notebooks were wedged between the dashboard and windshield along with a bottle opener, metal bottle caps, and a yellow pencil or two. Receipts for feed, scraps of paper, and candy bar wrappers were scattered all over the seat.

He would drop me off at the hog pens and "go see somebody 'bout something." I cleaned pens, cut lumber for stall repairs, nailed down loose tin on roofs, and fed by hand (my father hated anything mechanical that made life easier) over 700 hogs and pigs. Late in the evening I would see Big Green coming down the path in a cloud of brown dust.

I'd climb into the truck — sunburned and smelling of hogs and boy sweat. As I pulled the door closed my father would sing, "*See you later alligator!*" I would grin and shout, "*After awhile crocodile!*" Then down the road we would go singing at the top of our lungs.

Sometimes my father would act like he'd lost control of the truck. We'd both yell and then he would "regain control" and we would laugh and start the song all over again. Neither of us could carry a tune and really, neither one of us could drive. But we sang our song and we always made it to the house in time for supper.

Over the years it has occurred to me that people who have known hard work all love a good song, appreciate a hot meal, and never forget how to get back home.

Free Therapy and Inner Peace, Right Here!

Call me Joe the Barbarian but when I see the Hollywood people with their spiked hair, ten million dollar weddings, their need to be bigger than life, their sweaters made from harpy eagle feathers woven with organic peat moss, I want to grab my outdoor jacket, insulated jeans, and head to the mountains. The Blue Ridge Parkway is fifty-three minutes from my house, and I have an urge to go there, slog through snow covered woods, and hike to the top of a mountain, take in the splendor, and let my jangled soul find rest.

The urge hit me again recently as I crossed the scenic Catawba River on my way to a nearby city listening to a man on the radio talk about a book he had written as a form of therapy. He talked about an unhappy childhood, and as a result he became a transvestite, found he wasn't satisfied so he had a sex-change operation, which was a mistake and now he is back from a Malaysian lake where he went to seek inner peace but still has abandonment issues and blames his blue collar, insensitive father. Right there, just as I crossed the bridge over the Catawba River on Interstate 40 I said out loud, "Oh, grow up."

Yes, I talk to myself sometimes and if you live long enough, you too, will have that privilege.

Therapy is by nature a whiny process — high dollar whimpering, so I go the mountains and see what God is doing while everyone else gets the blues and takes decongestants.

My city is a wonderful place to live in with parks, beautiful homes, blueberry scones, and HD TV, and yet you can hop in your car and shortly find yourself in a silent snow covered mountain forest. Suddenly you are in Boris Pasternak's *Dr. Zhivago* waiting for Yuri (Omar Sharif) and his mistress Lara (Julie Christie) to come riding together through the woods in a sleigh all starry-eyed for each other. The moment you step into a winter forest you see the splendor yet sense the danger and you have a strong urge go in deeper.

You can blame your loving mother for this. She told you a million times never go in the winter woods alone, that the seemingly safe ice on a pond can break and you could fall in and be lost forever. Of course this enhances the experience and becomes something you must do. The danger is real, the snow is cold, and the laws of physics apply to us all. We need moments of splendor as well as danger to remind us that we are not the center of the universe and that one should never travel without wearing clean underwear.

Some time ago I took a guest from Brazil to the mountains. He had never experienced snow and ice. We tramped through the woods as a light snow fell. He kept grabbing at snowflakes. We arrived at a frozen pond, and I showed him how to step out on the ice. We both stood there and took in the silence, the majestic mountains, and the millions of snowflakes falling all around us.

He was speechless, almost childlike, and looked at me with a wide grin, his eyes watered from the cold, his nose running, and his ears red. He wanted to tell me how wonderful this was, but he couldn't describe it. We later walked back to the cabin saying nothing. We each felt small yet complete.

You don't have to go to half way around the world to find inner peace. Usually, it's where you're at, and it's free. Just stop and enjoy it.

For All the Waiting People of the World

I spent part of a rainy Saturday afternoon in a wonderful eatery called Groucho's Deli on Center and East Broad waiting for a friend. I sat by a window at one of those tables with the chairs higher than normal so you want to watch out and not be clumsy and fall and splat yourself on the floor. While I sat I drank hot coffee and watched the rain fall on the sidewalk as people walked by trying to avoid the small puddles that had started to form.

I didn't think about much else except where my friend was, and I hoped nothing bad had happened to him. Then I realized I should not worry too much. People today do not take time seriously and as a result a lot of other people's time is wasted — mine to be exact.

I sit in many meetings at church, school, work, committees, city council meetings and a homeowners' association and I wait on a lot of people that are late. I always do the calculations while I sit. If there are twenty people in a room waiting on you and you show up three minutes late you just wasted sixty minutes of human life — and we don't get it back ThankYouVeryMuch. What gives you the right to waste people's lives? And no, you're not that important. You knew you were supposed to be somewhere at a certain time, so grow up and shake a leg.

Big Decisions Are Best Made with Hotdogs

I stifle heavy sighs when the late party enters the room and acts as though they've just had to talk a Boeing 747 down from the sky and now they are trying to focus on the task at hand with the last of their remaining strength. A 7 p.m. meeting now starts at 7:15 and I miss *Survivor* on television.

If you're one of those that show up late and it's not your meeting and you interrupt twenty people you are not important — you're an Interruption. "Had to take an important phone call," you announce and lucky us, we get to see your new Brooks Brothers suit or Prada blouse and skirt as you fumble for a seat. The meeting was booked five days ago. Puhleeze!

Late Comers get a break the rest of us do not get — we've done a lot of the heavy waiting so *they* don't have to. Apologies are rarely forthcoming. It's like: if you do not apologize it means you're important. Bur remember, your mother taught you that is just plain inconsiderate. So grow up.

These days even friends do not bother to apologize for being late.

"Hi, I've been waiting for ten minutes — was worried about you."

"Oh, I was answering an email and got distracted by a comment about fruit co-ops in Brazil. What're you drinking — diet?" No apology or acknowledgement that they are late.

I think there should be a rule. If you can't haul your sweet self to a meeting at the appointed time, you pay for everybody's lunch the next day but first you have to find everybody because like a covey of spooked quail — we've flown.

We're at Groucho's Deli swinging from the chandeliers, dancing on tabletops with roses in our teeth and singing old sailor songs. Fifty-three people have formed a conga line that goes out the door and onto the street. Police sirens are wailing and someone's singing Little Richard's "Jenny, Jenny." Sweaters and ties are hanging on the overhead ceiling fans. We're laughing and having a ball because we're not waiting for a narcissistic personality to make a grand entrance. We, the Waiting People, have taken our lives back. Don't like it? We don't care. Turn up the music!

I wrote all of this on two napkins and drank one large decaf.

The Class of 1971 Has My Heart — and My Stomach

In 1769 Nicholas-Joseph Cugnot, a Frenchman, took off his beret long enough to build the first steam powered car and everybody thought it was totally tres bon until the early 1900s when Standard Oil of Ohio told everybody that gasoline was better. Henry Ford said, "No kidding?" and built thousands of gasoline powered cars, which created all over America the need for paved roads — one of which I followed to the Brook Valley Country Club in Greenville, NC. My forty-year high school class reunion had begun.

You go to high school reunions not to see old friends as much as to see what our teenage selves became as reflected back in the eyes of those that knew us when. So you can imagine my shock when I entered the room and noticed our teenage selves looked a lot like the teachers we use to have (Note: I for one always thought we had very nice looking teachers).

The first act of meeting an old classmate can be touching as you go for a warm handshake and realize your stomachs are almost touching, too. Your eyes are constantly glancing at name tags even though everybody tells each other that they've hardly changed a bit.

Big Decisions Are Best Made with Hotdogs

To be fair some truly had not changed much at all which I found to be as surprising as it was irritating. I tried to hold in my stomach.

The mood of the room was joyous as many could now afford a better grade of alcohol. The bar was doing a brisk business as "Joy to the World" (the one by Three Dog Night) blared out in a room that was a casserole of different conversations and sounds. There was the occasional shrill laughter as a group of women reacted to something said and you heard the hearty slap of a hand on the back of someone who recognized an old friend and a new conversation began.

In 1971 the barn doors swung open, they slapped our haunches with a diploma, and we galloped off into the world with our manes flowing and our heads held high. *Hawaii Five-O* and the *Mary Tyler Moore* Shows were favorites and the first Super Bowl to be played on artificial turf occurred with the Baltimore Colts defeating the Dallas Cowboys. John Denver sang to us about country roads and the Temptations decided love was just their imagination running away with them. I noticed a woman whom I carried a big torch for in those days had changed little and could pass for a mid-thirty while a former athlete walked with bad knees carrying about 200 additional pounds. I pulled my stomach in tighter.

We showed each other pictures of our kids and grandkids and the photos had to be held very still — under good light — at arm's length. Some laughed about it. I was getting dizzy. I really needed to breathe.

You learn that someone lost a child to a terrible accident, someone had beaten cancer three times, some were happily divorced while others had the same spouse they started with decades ago. The mood became relaxed, the lights were dimmed (slightly so we wouldn't fall) and the dancing began. My stomach resumed its natural shape and for a few hours the music carried us back to football games, proms, first kisses, and to each other.

They say the young today have everything — the chance of long health and amazing technology. But to never have danced to the Temptations song "My Girl" with someone you love is to miss a wonderful thing. The young — I almost feel sorry for them.

Blue Skies and Each Individual Leaf Is a Wonder

I am headed north on Interstate 77 crossing a bridge after having eaten grilled shrimp at a lakeside café on Lake Norman. I'm enjoying a gorgeous Indian summer day, which makes an old Baptist like me nervous. We fear temptation and spontaneity. I've a sudden urge to abandon all obligations and live in a commune by the lake whose members worship blue skies and forbid the use of clocks.

I have a mountain of work. My city job demands 24/7 of my time and by some misfire of my DNA, I also write a weekly newspaper column and short stories which all demands an equal amount of effort. I don't walk on beaches or sunbathe looking up into the sky, which right now is a beautiful Carolina blue. Only God could make a sky like that.

My gaze returns back to the interstate and I see rear red lights that are not moving — but I am. I apply the brakes and become annoyed at this sudden delay.

About a hundred feet ahead of me are blue lights and one of the northbound lanes is closed. There is an eighteen-wheeler lying on its side in the median and a crumpled small car, both doors open and bent, nearby.

Big Decisions Are Best Made with Hotdogs

A body lies covered in a white sheet.

Traffic crawls along and I come upon a scene of highway patrolmen in their black and grey uniforms and fire control people in bulky dark suits with bright reflector stripes on them. A small group of patrolmen move between me and the scene and the body is blocked from view. I see an officer talking, pointing to the ground, gathering evidence. I'm no longer disgruntled but now feel chastened, ashamed of my self-centered annoyance, and I am careful to look straight ahead and drive slow.

A Carolina blue sky over Lake Norman and boats are pulling skiers, young women in bathing suits walk along narrow beaches, joggers are out, and a kingfisher plunges into the water and arises with a small fish. Today you've seen sudden death and now life becomes a fragile lovely thing. You roll down the windows and breathe in the fresh air blowing from the lake and realize you've never seen trees and leaves like you do now. Each individual leaf is a wonder.

My home is tucked away in eastern Statesville, and I arrive to a house that somehow looks different from when I left this morning. I live here. That takes on a whole new meaning now.

I walk through the house and out into my fenced back yard, I just want to stand outside and appreciate everything — God, please help me be thankful — and suddenly eighty pounds of happy boxer comes bounding at me. For nine years she's greeted me almost every day wanting to play, but I usually just pet her head, say a nice word, and keep walking.

But today I face her and go into a crouched position. She's momentarily shocked, she stares, her tongue hangs sideways. Her expression says, "What's this? The chubby man never wanted to play before."

Then she grabs an old ball and I chase her around the yard. In thirty seven seconds we both collapse to the ground gasping for breath — I smile, scratch her ears, and look at her grizzled old face now bleached white by age. I hug her and we both roll over in the grass under Carolina blue skies. Keeping my dress pants and white shirt clean simply doesn't seem so important anymore.

Blue Skies and Each Individual Leaf Is a Wonder

The news says the truck driver's name was Richard. Did they call him Rick? Sorry you couldn't be here to play today, Rick. I'm so sorry you had to leave us.

The Taming of a Man

Years of research have shown that women have a civilizing effect on men. That idea sells a boatload of women's magazines.

Many believe that without women men would remain slobs and that our knuckles would still be dragging the ground. At some point a cavewoman gave a caveman a list of errands (pick up some milk and a rotisserie chicken at the T Rex Mart) and so he figured out a lot of things. Civilization with its paved roads, pick-up trucks, and forklifts is just the result of some poor man trying to get a wooly mammoth back home and into the freezer. Remember, she'd sent him for a chicken.

But the truth of the matter is men are still slobs; we just don't get to enjoy it.

My wife went out of town for a few days, and the house sprouted clothes like mushrooms after a rain. There were socks on the couch, shoes in the dining room, pants hanging on chairs, T shirts in the hall, and boxers in the refrigerator — just kidding — the boxers turned out to be my Beatles *White Album.*

A home is subject to the same laws of physics as the rest of the universe and when a stable body is removed a vacuum occurs and an ugly truth is revealed — the only body left in the house does not know where the laundry room is.

Big Decisions Are Best Made with Hotdogs

High school science teaches us that a body at rest tends to stay at rest unless a body close by reminds the first body that the garbage isn't going to take itself out. For men "at rest" is our normal state. Exceptions to this rule occur when men gravitate towards a smaller mass such as the remote or a bag of Doritos.

Men are like bears, loveable slobs of nature and we like to do what bears do. Left alone we'd amble about, swipe at a jumping salmon or two, rub our backsides against anything upright, and sleep all winter. We are not aggressive but we will shovel our driveway when it snows to show the other bear guys that we are alive and virile and don't mess with our honey bunch. On the other hand clearing the snow away makes it easier for other bear guys to come into your home — but then bear guys aren't noted for being real smart.

Men are by nature simply not civilized. We should never have put plumbing in the cave. Given our druthers toilet seats would not only be left up at all times, we'd just use the woods. We believe long pants at breakfast are not necessary and the only food that should never be barbecued on a grill is a six pack of your favorite beverage.

Like government bonds, we take awhile to mature, and if you bring us into a relationship patience on your part is required. It takes time for us to forget we used to scarf milk straight out of the carton, but now we should pour it into a glass. Shortly after we were married, my wife began training me with jelly glasses that had pictures on them. Every time I poured the milk into a glass with the funny pictures on it she would give me a piece of cheese. I was so proud.

A man needs a woman even more than he needs zinc or vitamin E. At times men grumble about domestication and howl into the dark but it's all bravado, Honey Cakes. Deep down men will embrace any rule and strive to do our best so long as we know this one thing about women — and that is that they love us.

Soap or Consequences

Recently I finished reading a delightful children's book written by an author/poet friend of mine, Dicy McCullough, titled *Tired Of My Bath*. It's a wonderful story of a little boy, John Allen, who did not want to take his bath and his mother warned him of the consequences. And guess what? The kid experienced consequences! I was amazed that the concept of allowing a child to suffer for his/her own actions was still considered. I swooned twice before finishing the book. These days, parents scramble to remove all obstacles that might hinder their child from experiencing the world and reality. I was raised on secondary smoke, beans and rice. These days, a guest who smokes is sent to the backyard like a convicted sex offender — can't have Johnny inhale anything stronger than his mom's Yankee Candle. If a kid misbehaves, parents desperately thumb through reference books on child rearing for the correct reaction to "when siblings express themselves." It's all about feeling good instead of learning responsibility. My mom would cut to the chase and whack the daylights out of you. I'm loaded with responsibility. Today, children are raised in the Home of Free Expression where discipline is rationalized away, and kids are served fast food eight out of seven days a week (yeah, I did the math and I stand firm).

Big Decisions Are Best Made with Hotdogs

Children are coddled to the state of an invalid and are rarely held to standards or made to suffer consequences. In my day it was wrong to treat a child as a helpless thing. When I was a kid instead of padding they had rocks under the city jungle gym sets. You learned to hang on. They didn't have safety belts on swings because the whole point of swinging was to see how high you could launch yourself upward, toward the sun — in free flight. Sometimes you landed on your shoulder or arm. You went to the emergency room just as soon as your mom went outside to hang the wash and found you flopping around like a fish. Emergency room nurses kept suckers to give you as soon as the doctor finished constructing your arm cast. It was okay in those days to give a kid sugar because nobody was hyper; spankings took care of that. We parachuted off the corners of our houses with pillow cases and tied towels to our back to act as capes (like Superman) and learned for ourselves that we cannot fly, no matter how loud we scream "Geronimo!" We threw dirt clogs and nails at each other, there was no such thing as sunblock, we played with BB guns because they could hurt you. We'd take turns shooting each other in the rear-end to see who would squeal first. We blew up model airplanes with M-80s, and our metal Tonka toys had cadmium in them. One time I swallowed a small plastic Roy Rogers canteen, my mother gave me castor oil to speed the passage of the object through my digestive system, yet still my mother made me eat my vegetables — to this day I've never received any counseling for that event. We rode our bicycles without helmets directly into traffic and built go-carts out of scrap wood and we drove those into traffic too. We soon learned the first name of every traffic officer. It was "Sir?" We played outside on the grass and invented games, and sometimes we got mad and settled things with fights and wrestling. Then we'd get over it and go play army and shoot each other with sticks for machine guns. But at day's end our mothers would always make us take a bath because if you didn't there were consequences — and no one wanted anymore of those than was necessary. Here's to you, John Allen.

(Dicy McCullough is also the author of *Tired of School, Tired of Being Different,* and *Tired of Being a Bully*)

Sir, Your Screams Are Forgiven

Sunday and I am driving through my neighborhood observing picturesque yards with thriving lush greenery, shrubbery, and multicolored flowers, the labor of each homeowner evident and offered for the viewing pleasure of any and all. Yet the children here could be living in quiet desperation, feeling abused for being pressed into labor back in April and May which in turn made for this beautiful yard. They want to tell their stories, maybe on Oprah, and watch camera close-ups of their parents explaining themselves. My son was also pressed into hard labor this spring and as a result is probably experiencing those same thoughts. I smile. This does not bother me. He will forgive me the day he makes his own son learn chores and the art of scooping dirt with a shovel.

I am on my way home from church, a place founded on forgiveness. And good stories. Today's story was about an adulterous woman and her accusers, the Pharisees, who wanted to stone her. She had made bad choices but our Lord forgave her, prevented the authorities from stoning her, and told her to go and sin no more. A story all too real that shows, among other things, people in authority can become calloused and willing to commit horrendous acts of cruelty.

Big Decisions Are Best Made with Hotdogs

The massacre in Houla in Syria comes to mind. About a hundred women and children, mostly children, were simply killed outright, executed so someone could make a political statement. The Syrian president claims the murderers were terrorists, their actions may signal the beginning of a civil war, and so he demands greater power. Hitler took the same tack with the "Kristallnacht" (Crystal Night) as an excuse for emergency powers, which ultimately led to the death of millions of Jews in the Holocaust. Interesting to note that when one person is attacked it is a story but when a hundred or millions are executed it is a statistic or an estimate. Man's heart is cruel and his mind thinks evil continually.

Which compels one to take a moment, a break from pondering man's cruel campaigns, and enjoy this quiet street and its green lawns, toys on a front porch, a cat slinking around some hydrangeas, a bicycle propped against a tree — it's the miracle of the everyday business of life, an uneventful day. Much of what the world seeks is represented here on this street — security, peace, prosperity, a bed of orange Day Lilies, a child's chalked message on a driveway. There are men who would destroy this on a whim and men who walk the wall at night to protect it.

But here today we are not interested in war or the politics of a corrupt Syrian or past dictators. Good stories all, but sometimes you wish people would put down their TV remotes and get angry about meanness and cruelty.

I think of the man on the interstate highway last week that became enraged when I changed lanes. I thought I had given him plenty of warning with my turn signal and lots of space but apparently he felt I had cut him off. He pulled up beside me, rolled his window down and screamed obscenities. Then, for emphasis, he showed me his one special finger, gunned his engine and cut in front of me, hit his brake lights several times, and then sped away out of sight. Later down the road I passed him parked on the road's shoulder making the acquaintance of a state highway patrolman.

I wish he could show some rage for those massacred children. I like to think that later he felt embarrassed, hoped none of his friends saw him so that when he pulled into his driveway and saw the chalk message "I love Daddy" and saw his house and its lush green yard and unharmed children running to meet him, that he felt chastened. I hope that he got out of the car and realized his home was as he left it this morning and took a moment to look at all that was his. I hope he went inside, kissed his wife, changed clothes, petted the dog, and went outside to set up the sprinkler. Earlier he wanted to stone me, but now with time to reflect I hope his rage is replaced by gratitude. I realize I have a responsibility myself, to forgive, even as I've been forgiven in the past.

    Good sir and father, thank you for your beautiful yard. I enjoy looking at it. Your family is safe and loved. Your crude public display of rage is forgiven. Now go, you blessed man, and scream no more.

Sex in the Secret Service Reminds Me of Superman

I've been trying not to think about the big party some Secret Service boys threw with the local prostitutes in Cartagena, Colombia and instead think about the future of American Chinchilla farming or about global warming, but it is hard to put tropical sex out of your mind. Besides — the environmental impact was slight, a few sheets and towels at most.

Our guys with the really dark sunglasses and black suits went to Cartagena to scout out the area before President Obama was to arrive a week later. No doubt the stress of operating in a tropical resort environment created a need to bond with some locals and swap jokes — Colombians tell the same jokes about Peruvians that Americans use to tell about Polish people — and they were all very happy about the FTA (free trade agreement) and thought they'd test the process out. But there was a misunderstanding about phasing out tariffs for goods and services and a prostitute thought it was $47 and an American agent thought it was $42 and the police were called and now the secret service man is listening to his wife's divorce lawyer explain why the wife is getting the house and the Volvo. Free trade has its pitfalls.

Big Decisions Are Best Made with Hotdogs

And that is about all we know except one Secret Service man is believed to have said, "My life is ruined." Which is the type of thing a good Protestant American boy should say after he has gotten drunk, had sex with a potential spy, and perhaps compromised the safety of the American president. It shows good manners. You can't have international sex with a complete stranger on company time and then say, "I had a mood swing." You're pretty much expected to tear at your clothes and go around in sack cloth and ashes.

Many people feel the need to go somewhere else to misbehave. I am a Baptist and therefore all forms of joy are suspect such as when my brethren tell me they are going to vacation in Cancun or the Bahamas supposedly for the gentle tropical breezes. "Gentle breezes for what?" one must ask. Ha! Wild sex and skipping bed time prayers, most likely.

This is one area of life American writers need to explore. You read about the Secret Service and their professional reputation and you think, "They would never do such a reckless thing as that. No way, no how, not those guys!" And so you write a story and attempt to create understanding by putting the reader into bed with the prostitute and write it as though the Secret Service agent was full of patriotism and sacrifice while his pants and drawers lay scattered on the floor of a five star hotel room. Don't over use the word "sweaty".

But this is what happens to a nation that has excused moral responsibility and bad behavior for so long the cancer has eaten its way to the top of what was once the very best. God is not mocked and the age of these men indicate they are the first products of that time when this nation first told God to get out of our schools and our laws.

Such behavior defies reasoning. I'm reminded of the time I was nine, tied a towel to my neck for a cape and jumped off the top corner of the house to fly like Superman. I landed in an old rose bush and was scratched badly and twisted an ankle.

My mother heard my screams and ran outside but stopped short upon seeing I was still alive and said, "What in the world were you thinking?"

Which is a good question to ask the Secret Service.

Please Tell Me Where Is Up?

There is a place that contains your golf club driver, your back-up set of car keys, the "other " sock, some dish towels, your metric #4 open face wrench, old high school picture albums, and when you need it the most — your check book. But you can't find them. You can't find them because you tried to improve yourself, tried to organize your life, to drive out that last remnant of a nomad wandering the earth. You sought to bring order out of chaos and so you decided to put things "Up."

But apparently Up is difficult to locate. Hitler's diaries were put Up for safe keeping and despite efforts by Soviet and American intelligence agencies, the documents are yet to be found. Someone put Jimmy Hoffa Up and no one has a clue where he is at the moment. Occasionally my wallet goes to Up along with my car keys. My wife and I were given a beautiful set of dishes for our wedding so we put them Up for safekeeping. They've not been seen for twenty-two years.

Up is a tough place to get back to. You can find Up easily enough the first time but returning back to it baffles entire governments, families, and individuals.

Big Decisions Are Best Made with Hotdogs

Recently I asked my wife where she put my pair of leather motorcycle gloves that were last seen lying on the kitchen counter by the breadbox.

"I put them Up," she said.

"So, they should be in the hall closet with my helmet, right?" I replied.

"Hmmm, maybe, but I know I put them Up." She said this while rattling through her kitchen cabinets looking for a nutmeg grater that she had put Up.

I walked to the closet, opened the door, and of course, the gloves were not there. Rumor on the street had it that the gloves had been seen hanging out together in the downstairs closet. However a quick follow up and search failed to find said gloves. To date, the gloves are still in Up.

One time my wife and I put Up our son David. He was almost three months old, and we'd both taken turns rocking him through several consecutive nights of colic. Nothing can make a baby cry like colic. Herding cats or putting a man on the moon is easier than dealing with a colicky baby.

We were bushed, frazzled, sleep deprived, and disgusted with the whole process of species survival — we'd come to believe it was way overrated. It was 5 a.m. and we were sitting on the couch and realized we had both fallen asleep sometime in the night, actually gotten a short nap. We stared at each other, two shell-shocked adults – the house was quiet. The silence was deafening but pleasant. We sat there a moment, relaxed. We actually began to smile.

Which of course felt wrong.

We were both a bit confused, sleepy but were fast becoming tense, the smiles leaving our faces. Our eyes began to take in the room, the furniture, the dim light of early morning, the patterns in the carpet, and the — baby. Where was the baby?

"I thought you were going to bring David downstairs," my wife said, groggily.

"Oh," I yawned. "I thought you put him Up."

"I thought you put him Up," she said.

We both snapped upright and alert. We looked at each other in horror.

"So?" She glared at me with one eyebrow arched high, "Does that mean he is in his crib, the basement, Montgomery Alabama — where?" Her voice had a shrill edge to it.

"I was so tired," I said. The days and nights had blended together. "He's upstairs." But my voice cracked with doubt.

We leaped from the couch, and like two stooges we tried to run upstairs at the same time. We wedged against each other shoulder to shoulder. We pushed, we jostled, we grunted, we elbowed each other, and we mumbled all the while our shoulders scrapped hanging pictures off the wall, decorative knickknacks were brushed aside and crashed at our feet. We had bad breath.

We raced each other all the way upstairs side by side until finally we reached the top and mercifully separated. My wife turned to the right, the direction to the crib, and I took a left to our bedroom. I heard my wife call out "He's not here! Where is my baby!?" I ran through the open door to our bedroom and pulled up short, relief washing over me.

Sure enough, God's-Gassy-Little-Angel-Sent-Straight-From-Heaven was right there in the middle of our king-sized bed, staring up at the ceiling with a big toothless grin on his round face, cooing softly to himself. He was checking out his fingers, one at a time. Our son had been put Up and by Divine Grace he had been found, with blankets like safety buffers bunched up around him. Up had been located — and it was our bedroom.

By now I had a bad headache and asked my wife where was the bottle of aspirin that had been on the nightstand beside our bed? Her brow wrinkled, she scratched her head in thought.

Yep, you guessed it, that had been put Up.

No, I'm Not William H. Macy

We've all experienced that moment — you're at one of those gatherings that occur during the holidays and you're standing in a small group of people discussing Peruvian pottery or gas mileage when a woman you do not know comes up to you and says, "Anybody ever tell you that you look like William H. Macy?"

There is something pleasant yet unsettling about being told you resemble someone else. When I was in college I wore wire rimmed glasses, had long hair, and I was sometimes confused with John Denver — until they heard me actually sing. But William H. Macy?

I couldn't place him right away so when I got home I Googled Mr. Macy and there he was — "Aha," I thought, "The movie *Fargo*. He played a character that had his wife kidnapped. He also starred in *Wild Hogs* and a slew of other movies. Macy has success, the annual income of a small country, and he doesn't pack his own lunch. Unless he writes a column and has a car with 165,000 miles on it, we have little in common."

I've always been shy and uncomfortable being me, so when I was young I loved masquerade parties at Halloween. Girls would dress up as royal princesses or fairies. Boys would dress as a zombie or smudge their faces and be a hobo or clown. One time I went as Edgar Allan Poe — dressed in a black suit, white shirt with a ribbon bow tie, and I wet my hair down and parted it to the side. To my disappointment people would walk by and call me Preacher. I was constantly trotting behind people explaining who I was and wishing I had a stuffed Raven glued to my shoulder. Appearances can lead to misunderstandings.

"To be great is to be misunderstood," said Emerson, which does not mean that if you're misunderstood you are great. Nope. We are all misunderstood most of the time. In my college days I wore bright colored bell-bottom pants and shirts open at the chest with billowy sleeves to declare my individuality — along with everybody else. Now I wear a shirt and tie with dress pants and impersonate someone who is gainfully employed. Either way strangers look at you and based on appearance, confidently come to conclusions about you that are totally wrong.

I am who I am — I made choices, we all make choices in life. Those choices are usually based on inaccurate information and so we end up being who we are. You reader: attractive, delightful personality with sharp wit, and good taste in reading material. Me: drops objects, bumps into things, forgetful, and shuffles when walking. Does it matter now? No, it does not. All a person really needs is to be understood and appreciated by two or three other people. Everyone else is just an audience, and we play to them until it's time for the curtains to fall. Humor and satisfaction are all in your head. Two people can be married for a glacier's age with all the joys, disappointments, and liver spots that come with matrimony and still look at each other and laugh and get excited. Anybody looking in from the outside would never understand.

Recently I came home from a long day at work, bumped into a foyer table, dropped the papers I was holding, and muttered under my breath. My wife, who was sitting downstairs called out, "Oh, I thought that sounded like you." And you can bet she didn't mean William H. Macy.

Mommies Make the Best Dancers

A Friday afternoon and the Food Lion parking lot was full of people hurrying to pick up groceries and get home to start the weekend. Earlier that morning the Carolina blue sky had promised a hot sunny day but now had turned bruised and heavy with rain. Clouds with dark stretched bellies bent lower to the ground.

In the South the likelihood of major weather events seems to trigger something in people. The southern herd bolts with the first rumble of thunder or announcement of snow and many head to the nearest supermarket just in case this turns out to be the very last day on earth you can buy food before the weather destroys our civilization and pounds us back into the ground from whence we came. It seemed that almost everyone in my city of Statesville, (population 26,000) had arrived at almost the same time. Car doors creaked open, people piled out of their vehicles and all hurried in mass before they were caught in what promised to be a thunderstorm you'd talk about later like the Mount St. Helens Volcano or the Great San Francisco Earthquake of 1906 — the Thunderstorm of 2012.

And there I was. Like everyone else I wanted to get in and get out before the storm really set in. There was a feeling in the air to rush, to be quick, and so I was threading my way through the crowd to the store's entrance when I first saw her.

She was a petite, blond haired mother moving through the crowd holding in each of her hands, the hands of two little blond haired girls, who looked to be about four and six years old. The giant herd of people had to split to go around them, some glared at the slow threesome while the mother, ever patient and taking small steps to match the children, held tightly to their hands and tried to hurry her little chicks along.

I came up behind them and was preparing to go around when I saw one of the girls break away from her mother, run a few steps ahead, turn back to face her family and say, "Mommy, I can dance! Watch!"

The mother was clearly in a hurry. The fact that she'd already had a long day was evident from the loose wisps of hair that fell down in her face, her white blouse that was slightly bunched having worked part way up and out of her belted cotton gray pin stripped skirt, and her black purse strap kept slipping down her shoulder and threatening to fall off at any moment. She walked like a lady that has been in heels and Hell all day — a tired slow walk, her feet seemed to be weighted down by her shoes. And now one of her girls has broken ranks and was making a demand that only a child, oblivious to life, schedules, pending weather events and high heels, could make. She wanted to dance.

To my amazement, in that panic hurried atmosphere, with people grumbling and rushing by and the smell of rain in the air — the mother stopped. I saw her glance up at what was now an almost black cloud overhead, look back at her angel, and nod to go ahead.

The result was a toothy grin from her daughter.

The child began to twirl and jump, shake her head, move her little hips, clap her hands, and turn around and around. She then did her version of a ballet ouvert, planted her feet carefully open then went into a move that could pass for a pirouette, completed the turn and stopped. She faced her mother and with her right arm across her waist, she bent low, faced the ground, and gave the traditional stage bow given by all professional entertainers.

Her mother clapped like a circus seal.

This produced a squeal from the sister. After some pleading and getting the okay from her mother, the second girl had her go at dancing. Her moves were similar to her sibling with each move maybe a bit more exaggerated. This was definitely a competition now. There was much twirling, some jumping, hand clapping, and hip shaking. At the end the same stage bow was given with much flourish and she ran up to her mother. Both girls had big smiles on their faces.

Then the one that appeared to be the oldest said, "You can't dance like that Mommy!"

I had now stopped completely still — caught up in their moment.

The mother looked at them and gave a dramatic show of surprise, as though told something that just wasn't so. She gasped and then said, "Oh yes I can!"

Honestly, the woman eyes looked like she was ready to fall down. I felt for her yet was amazed at how wanting to please someone you love can possibly break your ankles.

She took her purse off of her shoulder and laid it carefully in front her feet. She gave her girls a big smile and then right there in the parking lot dressed in her business grey, pin striped skirt, white blouse, and black high heel shoes the mother began to, well, er, dance.

Her black high heels made her legs a bit wobbly but she managed to turn completely around while waving her hands in the air (the Hokey Pokey?) and then she did a small tentative jump, wiggled her hips, and stomped her feet. She looked completely silly, totally uncoordinated, and so out of place.

Her girls broke out in squeals of laughter.

Their mouths flew open, their faces turned red, they laughed so hard they squatted down and slapped the pavement with their hands. They hooted and they hollered and they laughed at their mother. They mimicked some of the moves, complete with the wobbly legs, then giggled and laughed harder.

I thought, so that is what love sounds like.

They both ran up to their mother and hugged her around the waist. Their mother hugged them back, both at the same time which threw her off balance, almost fell from the effort, caught herself, picked up her purse, and then took both dancers by the hand and all three ladies resumed their walk towards the store. Their "mommy" had dropped the airs of an adult and entered the world of her children where there was no such thing as "hurry" and things like dancing, jumping, and laughing are to be done even in the face of a storm, maybe especially in the face of storms.

As I stood there and watched people bumped into me, my car keys fell out of my hand and onto the ground. Some people, annoyed at having to move around me cursed, and some muttered but I stood rooted to that spot. Big quarter size raindrops began to fall.

I felt buoyed by this experience, wrapped in a feeling of Good. I have no idea how many meetings and how much business that mother conducted that day, most of which she will not remember days, weeks, and months from now but that one moment she'll remember for the rest of her life. The rest of the crowd had hurried past, ignoring it all, too busy to see. My mind went back to earlier days.

My own son is now grown and I've spent most of my adult life in meetings that come with a public oriented government job. It brings home the bacon, puts gas in the car, and we can tip the pizza deliveryman. Most meetings are important, some involving millions of dollars worth of construction or materials, weeks of preparation and presentations and networking, but I can't recall a one single important meeting right now and I have twenty eight years of meetings to pull from.

But I can remember playing in the floor with a little boy and his Legos. I remember yelling at soccer games. I can remember and quote verbatim things my son said over fifteen years ago. I can not only quote them but can tell you the tone and timber of his voice when he said it. But I cannot remember what any of my very important business meetings to save my life.

I've never had a conversation with an elderly man or woman who told me about the meetings and jobs they had throughout their business career. Rather, they've told me about their children, their families, the little things like birthday parties, which kid put cereal in the dog's ears, or how could a kid get a pair of Cole

Palmer loafers down a home toilet? Those are things we remember, those sparkling moments of life, rare diamonds that we carry in our hearts' pocket all through our lives. But those meetings we think are so important turn out to have no more lasting value than disposable cups.

I resolved right then and there to go slow from now on. We assign importance to things that are so temporary and miss the things that will be eternal for us. It's quaint but it's true, slow down and smell the roses and you'll have time to dance in the parking lot.

It is rare an adult distills pure love in public, and I was lucky enough to see it happen. I suddenly felt lighter and as the raindrops picked up intensity I sashayed into the store.

Yes, it was a sashay, not a walk. I had no weight, I was feather light and as the two entrance doors slid open automatically I entered the supermarket and I found myself humming "Singing in the Rain." That's silly, you say. Bite me.

I danced my way over to produce, my shoulders moving and my waist bending. I used the corners of produce bins for support when I did a quick two-step move or a shuffle. I approached a shelf of canned goods, did a complete twirl, and deftly picked up a can of stewed tomatoes and plopped them into my shopping basket without breaking form. Oh, I had the moves.

I neared the herbs section, looking for fresh thyme where I was observed by an elderly lady. She watched me for a moment, then gave me a weak smile, reached over and grabbed some cilantro and then scurried away casting glances back over her shoulder. From there I tapped, shuffled, tapped and shuffled my way over to detergents.

I was humming a lot of John Denver but by the time I got to toiletries but I switched to James Taylor. He got me through sauces and condiments and "Carolina in My Mind" helped me pick out a rack of ribs.

I had a lot of shopping to do which gave me a lot of time to think. By the time I got to check out I thought it was a wonderful day to stand in line waiting for a cashier, and I told the lady beside me so and that we should all just take a moment and enjoy life and that I was thinking about taking up tap dancing. She stared at me for a moment then suggested that I move up in line ahead of her. "Please," she urged.

By the time I was ready to leave the store the storm had blown itself out and as I walked across the wet leaf strewn parking lot to my car I remembered my two-year-old granddaughter Chloe was coming over soon, tomorrow as a matter of fact. And right then, I decided, when she does get here, we were going to dance!